MAGIC IN
THE MOVIES
The Story of
Special Effects

MAGIC IN THE MOVIES

The Story of Special Effects

By Jane O'Connor
and Katy Hall

DOUBLEDAY & COMPANY, INC.
GARDEN CITY, NEW YORK

Library of Congress Catalog Card Number 79-7503
ISBN: 0-385-14716-3 Trade
ISBN: 0-385-14717-1 Prebound
Copyright © 1980 by Jane O'Connor and Katy Hall
All Rights Reserved
Printed in the United States of America
9 8 7 6 5 4

Library of Congress Cataloging in Publication Data

O'Connor, Jane, 1947–
  Magic in the movies: the story of special effects

  Bibliography: p.
  Includes index.
  SUMMARY: Discusses special effects used in films, including optical illusions, miniatures, and full-scale, live-action, weather, and makeup effects.
  1. Cinematography — Special effects — Juvenile literature. [1. Cinematography — Special effects] I. Hall, Katy, 1946 —   joint author. II. Title.
TR858.27   791.43'024

To Jim and Robby

To Jim

We wish to thank these people for their help in the preparation of this book: Linwood Dunn, Raymond Fielding, Orville Goldner, Jim Taylor, Ben Halpern, Matt Vogel, and Harry Madsen. We also wish to thank Mary Corlis and her staff at the Museum of Modern Art.

Contents

MAGIC IN THE MOVIES
The Story of Special Effects

1

What's So Special?

It might surprise you to know that the fierce tornado in *The Wizard of Oz* that swept up Judy Garland and deposited her in Munchkinland was nothing more than a woman's stocking with air blowing through it . . . or that Godzilla, the terror of Tokyo, was a man in a monster suit who went around stomping on toy-size buildings . . . or that wounded cowboys in black-and-white Westerns used to "bleed" chocolate syrup . . . or that the "lava" spewed forth by erupting volcanoes just might be cream of wheat!

Even the very first movies ever made were filled with special effects—tricks or illusions that fooled audiences into believing that they were seeing something they really weren't. As far back as 1893 shocked viewers of Thomas Edison's Kinetoscope (a type of peepshow machine such as those you might see at carnivals today) watched a realistic beheading in *The Execution of Mary Queen of Scots.* The little movie, which was less than a minute long, shows the queen kneeling at the chopping block. The executioner raises his ax and— whack!—off comes her head. Of course, horrified viewers never stopped to consider that the head they saw rolling on the ground belonged to a dummy which had been substituted for the live actress.

The primary purpose of special effects, however, is not to hood-wink gullible moviegoers but to give artistic freedom to moviemakers. Writers, for instance, have no limits on their imaginations.

Godzilla stops for a snack in a typical destruction scene from one of his many movies. (Toho Studios, 1954)

They can describe whatever they want and readers will see it in their minds. Film makers, on the other hand, must be able to show every event in a story on screen. Special effects help them to do this; special effects allow film makers to take any story, whether fantasy or fact, and transform it into a movie.

Whole worlds can be created through special effects. We witness things that never have been seen, like the band of friendly aliens in *Close Encounters of the Third Kind* (1977). Or real events that would be impossible to recreate can be simulated on celluloid—the burning of Atlanta in *Gone with the Wind* (1939), the sinking of the *Titanic* in *A Night to Remember* (1939), or the bombing of Pearl Harbor in *Tora! Tora! Tora!* (1970). Oddly enough, faking the destruction of the Hawaiian waterfront cost more than the actual Japanese invasion!

More often than not, however, the use of special effects cuts down production expenses. The famous director Cecil B. De Mille was known for making big-budget biblical epics like *The Ten Commandments* (1956) and *Ben Hur* (both a 1925 silent movie and a remake in 1959). Yet during the Depression even C.B., as he was called, had to watch his pennies. One movie that he directed called for a ship to catch fire at sea. Since it would have been far too expensive to set an actual ship on fire, a miniature was used. It was set afloat in a small tank of water. But the decks of the ship looked empty. De Mille insisted that somehow panic-stricken people had to be seen running around on board. At last a special-effects technician came up with an idea. Tiny paper cutouts of people were pasted to the backs of June bugs. The bugs were placed on the decks of the ship and it was ignited. The June bugs ran around in a complete state of frenzy and C.B. had his scene.

Another important reason for using special effects is that many natural occurrences—earthquakes, blizzards, and the like—are so unpredictable that the only practical way to show them on film is to fake them. In *The Good Earth* (1937), which is about a family of Chinese farmers in the early 1900s, a plague of locusts is seen swarming over the wheat fields. Since the movie was filmed in Hollywood, where locust plagues are few and far between, the only possible way to shoot the scene was to manufacture a swarm of insects. But how?

The solution was nothing short of sheer genius. A can of coffee grounds was poured into a tank of water. The swirling, floating grounds were filmed and then superimposed over scenes of the wheat fields. To moviegoers it appeared as if a black cloud of insects filled the sky. For close-up shots of the crops being devoured, dead "pickled" locusts were placed on the stalks of wheat and manipulated like little puppets with thin sticks stuck in their backs. The sticks were positioned so that they were never seen by the camera—or by the audience.

Special-effects experts may be called upon to do just about anything. Here, a crew member brushes up the shark star of Jaws. *(Photograph from* The Making of the Movie "Jaws" *by Edith Blake, copyright © 1975 by Edith Blake. Published by Ballantine Books, Inc. Reprinted by permission.)*

Special effects are also needed to simulate events that would otherwise be too dangerous to film. Without very clever movie magic, a skyscraper would never have been turned into a giant incinerator in *The Towering Inferno* (1974) nor would a mammoth quake have been able to rip apart Los Angeles in *Earthquake* (1974). In disaster movies like these, a director can rest easy knowing that when a day's shooting is done, there won't have been a single real fatality.

Of course, most special-effects work is not so splashy or spectacular. The everyday, run-of-the-mill techniques are merely supposed to enhance the reality of a scene. For example, artificial frost might

Actor Chris Reeves soars as Superman with some behind-the-scenes assistance from special effects. (TM and © 1979 DC Comics Inc.)

be painted onto the windows of a winter-cold house that is actually just a set inside a hot, lit-up studio. This type of trickery is meant to fade into the background. It is not supposed to call attention to itself. In fact, no special-effects work should ever upstage the story being told on screen.

And what of the people who create these wondrous illusions? Well, they tend to stay in the background, too. Today there are about two hundred special-effects men (women have yet to enter this field). Yet even though the "giants"—men like the late Willis O'Brien, who was the creator of the original *King Kong* (1933); John Dykstra, who engineered the thrilling dogfight that climaxed *Star Wars*(1977); or Arnold Gillespie, who whipped up the tornado in *The Wizard of Oz* (1939)—have provided some of the most memorable moments in movie history, their names are hardly household words. For many years, the work of special-effects experts was rarely even credited on screen because film companies didn't want to spoil the sense of realism for their moviegoing audiences.

It is true that, as with any magic trick, if we can see how a special effect is done, the illusion is ruined. Yet knowing what goes into an effect—for example, how Superman was made to fly or how the shark star of *Jaws* (1974) was created—does not spoil the fun. Rather, it makes us appreciate the expertise, imagination, and painstaking thoroughness of special-effects aces who may spend months and months to perfect a scene that takes up only a few seconds of screen time.

2

Focus on the Camera

Before *special* effects can be explained, it is important to understand how *ordinary* effects can be created with a movie camera. And before the workings of a movie camera can be explained, it helps to understand the way a still camera works.

A *still camera* takes snapshots or slides. It captures an instant of action and "freezes" it into a picture. A camera like this is basically a lightproof box. At the front of the box is a curtain-like device called a *shutter*, which, when shut, prevents any light from getting into the camera. But when a button on top of the camera is pressed, the shutter snaps open for a fraction of a second to let light into the camera. The amount of light that enters is regulated by the camera's *iris*. This iris works just like the iris or colored part, of your eye. It opens wide to let in lots of light on a dark day and closes down to keep too much light from entering on a very bright day. Behind the iris and the shutter is the *film*. Film is transparent acetate—a clear, plastic-like substance—that is coated with chemicals that change when they are exposed to light. The part of the film directly behind the shutter is the *only* part that is exposed to light when a picture is taken. Right in front of the iris is a window-like piece of glass called the *lens*. The purpose of the lens is to gather light from outside the camera and focus it on the film when the shutter snaps open.

If you want to take a picture, you look through your camera's *viewfinder* to get your subject into position. You hold your camera very still and press the *shutter release button*. The click you hear means that your camera's shutter has opened for a fraction of a second and snapped shut again. A lot happened during that fraction of a second. Light, reflecting from your subject, bounced through your camera's lens and its open shutter and hit the film. The chemicals on film react or "burn" depending on how much light hits them. This burning happens in the exact image of the object you are photographing. Light objects reflect a lot of light and they burn the film a great deal. Darker objects reflect less light and they do not burn the film so much.

As soon as you have taken a picture, you wind the film through your camera. The winding knob on the outside of your camera allows you to move the section of exposed film from behind the shutter onto the *take-up spool* and to move a new section of unexposed film into position behind the shutter. Now you are ready to take another picture.

After you have "shot" a whole roll of film, you send it to a lab to be developed. The exposed film is treated with chemicals to create a see-through piece of film called a *negative*. The exact picture you took appears on the negative, but in reverse. Light parts of your subject, which bounced a lot of light onto the film and burned it a lot, now look very dark. Dark parts, which did not reflect much light into the camera to burn the film, now look nearly transparent.

To get a finished picture, called a *print* or a *positive*, light is shone through the negative onto a sensitive piece of white paper, which turns dark when light hits it. When the negative is put *between* a bright light and the special white paper, the negative screens out some of the light hitting the paper. Where the negative is almost transparent, a lot of light gets through and turns the paper very dark. But where the negative is dark, hardly any light can come through it and so the paper stays white. What you have now is a *positive print* that looks just like the image you saw through your camera's viewfinder.

A *movie camera* works in basically the same way a still camera does. Believe it or not, it also takes *still* pictures. But the big difference is that a movie camera has a motor, which makes it possible for it to take many pictures, one right after another, in a very short time. Most movies you see in theaters are filmed with 35-millimeter

Negative of the Scarecrow from The Wizard of Oz. *(MGM, 1939)*

The positive print of the Scarecrow. (MGM, 1939)

movie cameras. The cameras get their name from the film they use, which is 35 millimeters (or *mm* for short) wide. It comes in strips, usually 1,000 feet long, and is wound onto a spool or reel.

Some 35-mm cameras have two large humps on the top that look like Mickey Mouse ears. The front "ear" holds the unexposed or "raw" film. The film travels from this *feeding reel*, through the camera and up onto the *take-up reel*, which holds the exposed film.

When a camera operator is ready to shoot some action, he presses a button which starts the camera's motor running, the shutter opening and closing, and the film moving through the camera. Everything is moving at an unbelievably fast speed inside the camera, but in order to understand what is happening, we'll take a "slow motion" look.

Once the motor is on, the film is pulled through the camera by the *sprocket wheels*. These wheels are edged with small teeth that fit into the holes—called sprocket holes—along the side of the film. These sprocket wheels do not turn smoothly, but move in tiny jerks, starting and stopping, starting and stopping, and so they pull the film through the camera in this start-and-stop way. The jerking movement of the film is hooked up to the opening and closing of the shutter. While the shutter is closed, the film jerks forward. As soon as the film comes to a stop, the shutter opens and exposes a small section of the film to light. (If the film were moving when the shutter snapped open, the image could not be clearly burned onto the film. The result would be a blur, similar to what would happen if a canvas were pulled out from beneath a painter's brush.)

After a section of film has been exposed to light and the shutter has closed once more, the sprocket wheels jog forward again. They advance the exposed area toward the take-up reel, and they pull a new, unexposed area of film into ready position behind the shutter. Again, the film stops, the shutter opens, and another image is captured on film. Each of these images is actually a tiny still photograph called a *frame* of film. A movie camera operates so fast even at normal speed that it takes 24 of these frames every second!

So, what a movie camera actually does is to break down movement into a *series of still pictures*. The scene of car chase, for example, might take 60 seconds to photograph. On film, this chase would be broken down into 1,440 separate frames (24 frames per second × 60 seconds = 1,440 frames). Most professional movie cameras come equipped with counters so that film makers can tell how many frames of film or feet of film they have taken of a given scene.

When an entire reel of movie film has been shot, it is sent to a lab to be developed. First, it is treated with chemicals to make a *negative*. This negative is used, much in the way the still-photograph negative was, to make a *positive print*. This positive print is actually a long ribbon with thousands of small pictures on it. But it looks nothing like a movie — yet. What is needed to transform this strip of photographs into action on the screen is a *movie projector*.

The purpose of a projector is to project or "throw" the pictures on the film onto a screen and to magnify them into huge images that fill the screen. Film travels through a movie projector in almost the same way it travels through a movie camera. The positive print — still called *film* — is held on top of the projector on a feeding reel and is threaded through the projector and onto a take-up reel. When the projector motor is turned on, sprocket wheels move the printed film through the projector in the same start-and-stop way that they moved the raw film through the camera. The projector, too, is equipped with a shutter, which opens and closes 24 times each second. Every time the shutter opens, a new frame of film has advanced to the "stop position" in back of it. A powerful projector light behind the film shines *through* the film. This projector light picks up the tiny image on a frame of films and beams it through the projector's shutter and lens. The lens magnifies the image thousands of times and focuses it on the huge movie screen.

Each frame is projected onto the screen for just the split second that the shutter is open. As soon as the shutter closes again, the image is blocked from the screen and, for a fraction of a second, the screen is completely dark. Then, inside the projector, the sprocket wheels move again and a new frame of film is advanced into place behind the shutter. The shutter opens, allowing that frame to be projected onto the screen. This happens over and over, 24 times each second and literally thousands of times during a movie.

But why, you may be wondering, do you see *action* on the screen instead of a series of still pictures? And why don't you see the dark screen during the split-second pause between frames?

The reason is that when your eyes see an image, the image is "held" in your mind for about a tenth of a second after it has actually disappeared from view. While you are watching a movie, each frame you see persists, or is held, in your mind and overlaps with the next frame on the screen. Because your mind has this blending ability,

Notice the very slight difference in the position of the falling man from frame to frame in this strip of film from The Great Train Robbery. *(Museum of Modern Art/Film Stills Archive)*

known as *persistence of vision*, you actually *see* fluid motion on the screen and not thousands of individual pictures. And, because your mind can blend these pictures together, you are not aware of the dark screen between the frames. If the frames were projected more slowly, you *would* see still pictures and the dark screen in between, just as you do when you watch a slide presentation. But movie film, projected at the rapid rate of 24 *f*rames *p*er *s*econd (or 24 *fps*), appears as motion.

This rate of 24 fps, by the way, is determined not by our persistence of vision, but by the *sound track*, which is printed along the side of a strip of film. It must pass through the projector's sound equipment at this 24 fps rate of speed in order to give good sound reproduction. Silent films were photographed at much slower speeds — 16 to 18 fps — and they still gave the impression of fluid motion on the screen.

You have witnessed the phenomenon of persistence of vision if you have ever flipped the pages of a "flip book." Flip the pages slowly and you will be aware of the many separate pictures. But if you flip them very quickly, the images on each page will persist in your mind, overlapping one another, and you will actually *see* the illusion of motion.

With the basic idea of the way a movie camera works in ordinary ways to make ordinary moving pictures on the screen, it's much easier to understand the *special* effects that a movie camera can create. And so on to the magic and illusion in the world of photographic effects.

3

Optical Illusions: Photographic Special Effects

Thomas Edison invented the movie camera, but it took a magician, Georges Méliès of France, to see how the camera could create fantastic illusions. In the late 1890s, Méliès bought a movie camera—a brand-new invention at this time—and went out to photograph the street life of Paris. He set up his camera stand, so the story goes, and began filming traffic on a busy street. Just as he was photographing a bus passing by, his camera jammed. When at last Méliès got the camera working again, the bus had gone and a hearse was traveling down the street. Méliès filmed the hearse and several other vehicles without thinking too much about the camera jam. But when he developed the film and projected the traffic scene onto a movie screen, he got a big surprise. He saw a bus rolling down the street and then —presto!—right before his eyes it turned into a hearse! Purely by accident, Mèliès had created the very first photographic or optical special effect.

An *optical effect* is a special effect created photographically. By manipulating a movie camera during the filming of a scene—for example, stopping it and then starting it again or changing the speed at which the film runs through the camera or covering up part of the camera's lens—many astounding effects can be created. Optical trickery may also be performed *after* a scene has been filmed, in a photographic lab, where the movie film itself is manipulated—layered together or even painted by hand a frame at a time.

Méliès wasted no time adding trick-photography films to his magic shows. Within a year of his lucky accident, he made seventy-eight short films—including the first vampire movie! In 1899 he made *Cinderella*, and he used his bus-into-hearse trick to help Cinderella get to the ball. He began by filming a pumpkin. Then he stopped his camera, which was kept very still. The pumpkin was removed from the scene and a fancy coach was put in exactly the same spot. Now Méliès started filming once more. On screen, the pumpkin was magically transformed into a coach. This simple optical trick is known as *stop-motion photography*.

With some help from a fairy godmother and stop-motion photography, Méliès magically transformed a pumpkin into this handsome coach in Cinderella. *(Museum of Modern Art/Film Stills Archive)*

John Barrymore as the villainous murderer in the 1920 version of Dr. Jekyll and Mr. Hyde. *(Museum of Modern Art/Film Stills Archive)*

It was stop motion that helped Dr. Jekyll turn into Mr. Hyde in the 1920 version of the film. *Dr. Jekyll and Mr. Hyde* is Robert Louis Stevenson's classic story of a kindly doctor who invents a potion which accidentally turns him into a crazed murderer. The first Jekyll-to-Hyde transformation scene in the film occurs after the good doctor mixes an unknown potion in his laboratory. Glass in hand, Dr. Jekyll sits down behind his desk. Slowly, he brings the foaming concoction to his lips. He hesitates slightly, then drinks it down. A look of horror crosses Jekyll's face. He reels from the effect of the drink and then faints, just managing to grab the edge of the desk with his hand as he falls. Suddenly, Jekyll's hand takes on a monstrous appearance, with long, claw-like nails, gnarled fingers, and ugly patches of hair. Then, up from behind the desk rises the hideous Hyde!

The star of this film, John Barrymore, was known for his convincing performances, but to turn from Jekyll to Hyde he needed a bit of help from the makeup artist as well as from the cameraman. When Barrymore, as Jekyll, fell behind the desk, the camera—a specially

Lon Chaney, Jr., son of the silent-film star, is transformed into the Wolf Man, his most famous role. (Copyright © Universal City Studios, Inc. All rights reserved. Museum of Modern Art/Film Stills Archive)

weighted one that would not move at all—was stopped. A film-crew assistant lightly traced the outline of Barrymore's hand on the desk. Then Barrymore went off to have his Hyde makeup applied to his hands and face. When it was finished, Barrymore returned to his position behind the desk, placing his now ghastly hand exactly where it had been before, and the assistant erased the outline. The camera rolled again and Barrymore rose up off the floor as the demented creature Hyde.

A variation of stop-motion photography helped to transform Lon Chaney, Jr., into a fiend in *The Wolf Man* (1941). Chaney played the role of Lawrence Talbot, a young student who wanders about the barren Transylvania landscape on the night of a full moon and is bitten by a werewolf. Talbot knows that with the coming of the next full moon he, too, will become half man, half wolf. Sure enough, as the light of the full moon shines on Talbot, the clean-shaven student gradually sprouts hair all over his face and his teeth lengthen into gleaming fangs; he is, indeed, a werewolf.

Lon Chaney, Jr., might have found his man-to-monster transformation more pleasant if he *had* been bitten by a werewolf! At least it would have been a speedier process. To effect the change, Chaney had to stand in one spot, looking directly into the camera. The back of his head was supported by a brace which held it perfectly still. Then a cameraman—again using a super-heavy immovable camera—shot a few frames of film of Chaney as Talbot. The camera was stopped and the makeup crew stepped in. They glued a few pieces of hair—yak hair, in fact—one strand at a time to Chaney's face and hands. Then they stepped back out of the way and the cameraman shot a few more frames of film. Again, the camera was stopped and more hair was pasted to Chaney. This tedious procedure happened over and over and over until, at last, Chaney was the complete werewolf. This "hair-raising" transformation actually took a grueling seven hours to complete, but on screen it took only ten seconds!

FAST AND FURIOUS

In the early days of the movies, camera operators cranked the film through the cameras by hand. When Mack Sennett, later known as the King of Comedy, began directing silent films, he was very short on money. One day, so the legend goes, Sennett decided that he was spending far too much money on film and he told his cameraman to crank the film through the camera very slowly in order to use as little of it as possible. So the cameraman cranked slowly as he photographed cars rolling down the street and actors walking on a sidewalk. After the film was developed, it was projected at normal speed (about 18 frames per second for silent films) and Sennett could hardly believe what he saw. Automobiles appeared to be zooming at a hundred miles an hour and people jerked along the sidewalk at breakneck speeds! The entire scene looked as though it had been filmed on a planet where everything happened many times faster than it did on Earth. Sennett, in an attempt to cut costs, had stumbled onto the technique of *fast-motion photography*.

Fast motion works this way. If Sennett, for example, directed an actress to heave a custard pie at one of his Keystone Kops, she would draw her arm back, throw the pie, and watch as it splattered in the face of the surprised cop. The entire action might take 4 seconds. A camera, shooting at the average 18 fps speed for silent movies, would film this pie throw on 72 frames of film (4 seconds × 18 fps = 72 frames). If this film were then developed and projected at the regular speed, which, by the way, always remained constant at 18 fps, the pie throw would take exactly 4 seconds of screen time (72 frames ÷ 18 fps = 4 seconds) and would appear to be happening at normal speed. But, if this same pie throw were shot by a cameraman cranking the film through the camera at only *half* speed — or 9 fps — the action would be photographed on just 36 frames of film (4 seconds × 9 fps = 36 frames). If this film were then developed and projected at the usual 18 fps speed, the pie throw would take only *2* seconds on the screen (36 frames ÷ 18 fps = 2 seconds). In other words, when the film moves through the camera *half* as fast, the action projected on screen appears to be happening *twice* as fast!

Sennett, like Méliès, knew how to make the best of a fortunate accident. His zany comedies were filled with mad car chases and scenes of rampant destruction, all done using fast-motion photography. A typical car chase might begin with fifteen Keystone Kops jammed into a paddy wagon in hot pursuit of a villain's vehicle. The cars might crash through a brick wall, skid crazily around a corner, barely missing two men carrying a sheet of plate glass, swerve and knock down a ladder, leaving a sign painter dangling from a billboard,

The Keystone Kops take a turn, undoubtedly for the worse, in one of Mack Sennett's silent comedies. (Museum of Modern Art/Film Stills Archive)

and zoom off a pier into the ocean for a grand finale. Sennett used fast-motion photography to film these wild chase scenes (actually the cars weren't going all that fast) with cameramen "undercranking" the film through their cameras.

Of course, movie cameras today aren't cranked by hand, but are motor-driven. The speed at which film travels through the camera can be regulated by a cameraman simply turning a dial to the desired number of frames per second. But even though a cameraman only has to set a dial to shoot fast-motion scenes, shooting at speeds below normal is still fondly referred to as "undercranking."

SPEED IT UP TO SLOW IT DOWN

On screen, slow motion creates just the opposite effect from fast motion: instead of being fast and jerky, slow-motion scenes look fluid and dreamlike. Not surprisingly, slow motion is created in exactly the opposite way from fast motion.

Say, for example, that a football player throws a pass that takes 2 seconds to complete. At normal camera speed for the sound movies of today, the pass would be photographed at 24 frames per second or in 48 separate frames (2 seconds × 24 fps = 48 frames). If this scene were projected at the standard rate, which is *always* 24 fps for sound movies, and never varies, it would also take 2 seconds of screen time and the pass would appear at its natural speed. But, if this same pass were photographed at *twice* the normal speed — as it frequently is in "instant replay" scenes — at 48 fps, the pass would be filmed on 96 frames of film (2 seconds × 48 fps = 96 frames). The action of the pass filmed at this speed would be broken down into *twice* as many frames as usual. If these 96 frames of film were developed and projected at the normal rate, it would now take 4 seconds of screen time (96 frames ÷ 24 fps = 4 seconds). So, in order to slow down the motion of the screen by *half*, the film must travel through the camera *twice* as fast.

Slow motion is a favorite technique of moviemakers who specialize in bloody battles. When they shoot a grisly fight scene in slow motion, they can be sure that you won't miss a single gory detail! Bruce Lee, of *Fist of Fury* fame, was always miraculously transported to a slow-motion world once he started delivering his deadly Kung Fu blows. Accompanied by bone-crunching sound effects, these heavy-duty fight scenes are not actually as hard to watch as they otherwise might be, because the slow motion gives them such an unreal — almost ballet-like — quality.

HIGH ADVENTURE

The scene is a skyscraper fire raging out of control. The action calls for a woman to plunge from the thirty-fifth floor of the blazing building. The film crews stand by. On a signal, the fires are ignited, the cameras roll, and the stunt woman portraying the unfortunate victim leaps from a flame-filled window and falls 32 feet—onto a safety mattress out of the camera's view.

This horrifying leap may actually have lasted for only a second. If it was filmed at the normal 24 fps speed and projected at the normal speed, the leap would also take one second of screen time. But, if the cameraman filmed the leap at a *faster* than normal speed—say, 96 fps —this would have the effect of stretching out the leap on screen and making it look even longer and more dangerous.

This technique, called *high-speed filming*, is achieved exactly the same way as slow motion. The difference between the two effects is this: *slow motion* looks slowed down, languid, and dreamy on the screen, while *high-speed filming* is used to trick the audience into believing that they are seeing *normal* motion on the screen.

ONCE IS NOT ENOUGH

Late-night TV movies abound with ghosts—those semi-transparent figures that may appear out of nowhere (thanks to stop-motion photography), walk through a few closed doors, and then, just as suddenly, disappear. Often these spirits are the result of an optical trick called *double exposure*.

To make a ghost walk right through a cemetery wall, from one side to the other, a camera is set up so that both sides of the wall are visible. The cameraman then exposes, say, twenty feet of film of just this wall. (Film is talked about in *feet* rather than frames when so much film is used that it would be awkward to talk about a huge number of frames. There are 16 frames to one foot of movie film.) Now the cameraman winds the twenty feet of film *backward* in the camera. There is a footage counter on the camera so that he knows just how far to rewind the film. The same twenty feet of film are now ready to be exposed *again*. The camera is taken to another set at this point and the actor playing the ghost is filmed—on the same twenty feet of film—simply walking across the set. Now the twenty feet of film has been exposed to light two different times. It has been *double exposed*.

The scene that was filmed first—the cemetery wall—"burned" its image onto the film and, on screen, it will appear as a solid image. The scene that was filmed second—the walking ghost—was photographed with the camera's iris closed down, letting less light into the

A ghost appearance by Joan Blondell in Topper Returns. *(United Artists, 1941)*

camera, and so the image is fainter, and appears translucent on the screen — just the way a ghost should look.

DISSOLVING THE INVISIBLE MAN

Movies sometimes begin with a dark scene that gradually gets lighter and lighter until it is correctly lit. This technique is often used by film makers to bring the audience slowly into the opening action of a picture. Such a transition is called a *fade-in*. To do a fade-in, a cameraman simply begins filming with the camera's iris closed. Then, gradually, as he keeps filming, he opens the iris wider and wider until the correct exposure is reached. At the end of a movie or the end of a scene, just the opposite effect is sometimes wanted — a *fade-out*. To achieve a fade-out, the camera operator closes the iris slowly, cutting out the light hitting the film until it is totally dark.

To get from one scene to another, a film maker will sometimes do a fade-out on one scene and then rewind the last several frames of that scene in the camera. Then he will do a fade-in on the next scene. On the screen, the first scene slowly fades away while the second scene slowly comes into view. This technique, of a fade-in double exposed over a fade-out is called a *dissolve*, which describes just what it looks like on the screen — one scene dissolving into another.

The Invisible Man (1933), starring Claude Rains, used dissolves in a remarkable way. This picture is about a scientist who develops a secret formula that makes him invisible. Unfortunately, the formula also makes him go crazy and he decides to use his power of invisibility to destroy the world. At the end of the movie, however, good prevails over evil: the Invisible Man, mortally wounded, is stopped from completing his mission. Lying on his deathbed (it is obvious that there is a body in the bed because there is a dent in the pillow and the sheets seem to be covering the shape of an unseen body), the Invisible Man slowly becomes visible. At first, only a faint ghost of a skull appears on the pillow. Then, little by little, the face takes shape and at last the face and body of the Invisible Man are clearly seen. (This was the first — and also the last — time in the film that Claude Rains's face appeared on screen.)

This death scene was accomplished by a series of dissolves and some clever substitutions while the camera was stopped between shots. At first, the Invisible Man's "pillow" (made of plaster and permanently indented) and his sheets (made of molded papier mâché) were filmed and then the cameraman did a fade-out. The film was then wound backwards in the camera. During this time, an actual skeleton was slipped into the body-formed sheets and a human skull was placed on the pillow. Now the cameraman faded in on the scene again for a few seconds and then faded out. The film was again rewound in the camera several frames and the skull and skeleton were replaced by a very bony dummy. The process was then repeated. For each segment in this scene, the camera faded in and faded out on a more human-looking dummy until at last Claude Rains took his place beneath the sheets for the climactic moment.

Although this was one of the most dramatic screen death scenes ever, the Invisible Man didn't stay dead for long. A series of sequels, including *The Invisible Man Returns* (1939) and *The Invisible Man's Revenge* (1943) proved him to be alive and well!

Split screen is a technique that is often used in films when an actor is playing identical twins. In such movies, the "twins" *must* appear in a few of the same scenes to convince skeptical audiences that the role is *not* being played by just one actor.

Imagine that a director wants to film "twins" walking down a path toward the camera. First the right side of the camera's lens is covered up by a card called a *matte card*. This will prevent any light from hitting the right side of the film. Only the *left* side of each frame of film will be exposed to light. Then the actor is told just where to walk for the scene. A special line is indicated on the set and the actor must not cross over this line. If he does, part of his body will not be filmed; it will be blocked out by the matte card. On screen, he would appear to be missing the part of his body that had crossed the line, so the actor must be very careful to stay on the *right* side of the set. As soon as this part of the scene is filmed, the actor goes back to his original starting place—but this time he stands on the other side of the set. The film, meanwhile, is wound backward in the camera and the matte card is flipped so that it covers up the left side of the lens. The *right* side of the film is now ready to be exposed. The actor enacts the same scene again, only this time he's careful to stay to the left side of the line. As the film runs through the camera, it photographs the actor on the other side of the set. The part of the film that was exposed the first time will not be double exposed because it is covered by the matte card and no light will hit it. When this finished scene is developed and projected onto a screen, ideally it will look as though a pair of identical twins were walking down a path, side by side.

A camera operator must be very careful where he puts a matte card so that a line won't show up on the screen. Sometimes the place where the two mattes come together can be lined up with a natural edge in the scene—a telephone pole, perhaps, or the corner of a building. Another way to hide a "matte line" on a plain background is to make sure that the matte card is just the right distance from the camera's lens so that it is slightly out of focus and fuzzy. Two soft, out-of-focus edges will blend together on the screen so that no matte line is visible.

The ultimate 1950s sci-fi thriller, *Forbidden Planet* (1956), used split screen for another purpose, but the principle was the same. The script called for a tiger to leap from a cliff and attack the captain of a spaceship. The captain had to turn, see the lunging beast, draw his trusty ray gun and—zap!—the tiger was supposed to be instantly vaporized. There were several obvious problems in shooting this scene as it was written. First of all, it would have been terribly dangerous to have an actual tiger jump at an actor and, secondly, how do you vaporize a five-hundred-pound tiger into thin air?

Split screen solved the problem nicely. First the left side of the camera's lens was covered by a matte card and the camera was focused on a tiger ready to leap from a cliff. The camera was positioned so that, mid-leap, the tiger would cross the matte line and, from the camera's point of view, simply disappear. Then the matte was flipped to the right side of the lens and the film was rewound "to heads"—or back to the starting point—in the camera. Now the space captain was filmed on the left side of a set that was built to blend perfectly with the tiger-and-cliff set. On cue, the captain turned, looked startled, whipped out his ray gun and fired—at thin air. On the screen, the two halves of the scene fitted together exactly and, just as the captain shot, the tiger appeared to vanish from sight.

BEHIND THE ACTION

Split screen is one way of combining two separate images and making them appear to be part of the same scene on screen. Another way of doing this is to use a technique called *rear projection*.

Rear projection made possible a famous scene from Hitchcock's *The Birds* (1963) that shows a group of schoolchildren running and screaming as birds—which have suddenly turned vicious and are attacking an entire town in droves—peck violently at their heads.

To create this horrible spectacle, Hitchcock first sent a film crew out to photograph some birds "attacking." From high atop a cliff, a crew member tossed out food to hungry birds. Below, a cameraman filmed the birds as they swooped and dove for their food. This film footage was taken to a photo lab, where it was developed.

Rear-projected "killer birds" dive and strike as kids run in front of a rear-projection screen for Hitchcock's thriller, The Birds. *(© 1963, Alfred Hitchcock Productions; Universal Pictures, an MCA, Inc. Company)*

The developed print was then taken to a movie set and threaded into a special movie projector located *behind* a movie screen made of a kind of see-through plastic. The projector was equipped with a very strong projection light and it projected the film of the swooping birds *through* the back of the screen so that the image showed up clearly on the front of the screen.

Hitchcock then began rehearsing the actors who played the children in front of the screen as the film of the birds was projected behind them. The kids learned to duck just as an angry bird appeared to peck them on the head. When the rehearsal was smooth, a camera in front of the children and the rear projection screen filmed the entire scene — with spectacularly frightening results.

The thing that makes rear projection work is that the projector behind the screen and the camera in front of the screen are hooked up to a "synchronizer" so that their shutters open and close at exactly the same time. As the projector's shutter opens and throws one frame of film onto the rear projection screen, the camera's shutter snaps open and photographs that frame along with the live action. This process continues for frame after frame of film. If the synchronizing were off just slightly, the camera would photograph the between-frame dark places and the result would be a terrible background flicker.

Rear projection was popular in Hollywood for a long time and is still used frequently. The problem with it is that if it is not handled just right, the result is a very obvious faked shot. Also, many times the projector behind the screen doesn't throw a strong enough image and the background appears to be much dimmer than the foreground live action.

IT'S A BIRD! IT'S A PLANE!
IT'S . . . FRONT PROJECTION!

Today *front projection* is often used instead of rear projection. With this method, the projector is placed in front and to the side of the screen. It doesn't project directly onto the screen, but it throws its image into a mirror that is set up at a 45° angle to the screen. The footage from the projector hits the mirror and is bounced onto the screen. Because of the angle of the mirror, actors in front of a front projection screen won't cast shadows that could be picked up by the camera.

The front projection screen itself is amazing. It is coated with millions upon millions of the tiniest glass beads imaginable — the kind used on highway signs to reflect lots of light from car headlights. These glass beads produce an incredibly clear and bright image for the camera to pick up, which gives this technique an edge over rear projection. Also, front projection can be used on a much bigger screen than can rear projection.

In the movie *Superman* (1978), the Man of Steel did much of his flying courtesy of front projection. Chris Reeves, in his Superman suit, was suspended in front of an 80-foot-wide front projection screen. Reeves could turn slightly in one direction or another or tilt his body up or down, but it was actually the front-projected images that did the "flying." Aerial views of New York City—standing in for Metropolis—were shot by helicopter and then this footage was developed and threaded into a front-projection projector. The projector beamed these vistas onto the huge screen and, by way of a complex system of zoom lenses, Superman seemed to be flying toward the audience or away—even though he was really just "hanging around" in one spot.

Many a ride-'em-down, shoot-'em-up movie of the Wild West has been filmed in the not-so-wild back lots of Hollywood studios. There, scenic designers can have a believable ranch constructed; prop men can bring in truckloads of cactus and sagebrush; and wranglers and horses can be hired. But if the script calls for a high, snow-capped mountain peak in the distance, the snowless Hollywood hills in the background just won't do.

A snowy mountaintop *can* be added to the Hollywood hills by a technique called a *glass shot*. A glass shot is just what it sounds like—a scene shot through a sheet of glass. On the glass is painted whatever has to be added to the scene—some clouds, perhaps, and the lofty mountain peak.

A glass shot is set up in this way. First, the camera is positioned exactly where it will be when filming the scene. Then a large sheet of glass, approximately three feet by four feet in size, is set up about six feet in front of the camera. Both the camera and the glass must be anchored rigidly so that neither of them will move even a fraction of an inch. Now, a special glass artist is called in to paint the mountaintop on the sheet of glass and to make it look as though it is a part of the overall scene. The artist begins by looking through the camera's viewfinder to see just where the mountaintop should go. He will then do some sketches on the glass while an assistant remains back at the camera's viewfinder to direct him so that he won't have to continually run back and forth from the camera to the glass.

When the sketch is finished, the artist will look at it critically from the viewfinder and make any necessary changes. Now he begins the actual painting in flat oil paints, which will stick to the smooth surface of the glass. The artist will check his progress occasionally through the viewfinder to make sure that the painting is lining up perfectly with the other elements in the scene. He will want to blend the bottom of the actual Hollywood hills into the base of his mountain, so that no one seeing the finished movie will be able to tell where the hills end and the mountaintop painting begins.

When the painting is finished, a "slop test" is made. That is, several feet of film are shot of the scene through the glass painting. This exposed film is taken from the camera and developed on the spot. The glass artist, the director, and the camera operator are accustomed to looking at the developed strip of negative film that results from a slop test, and they can tell how well the painting is blending in with the rest of the scene.

If all the elements match in the test, it's time for action. Actors take their places on the set. They are warned by the director not to walk or ride their horses into certain areas of the set, or their heads might be hidden from the camera by part of the mountain painting. On screen, a cowpoke who rode too far in the wrong direction might appear to have suddenly "lost his head" in back of a mountain peak that is supposed to be several miles behind him.

BRUSHING UP ON MATTES

Another way to combine two or more separate images to make them appear as part of the same scene is to use a live-action shot with a *matte painting*. A matte painting was used to heighten suspense and terror in *The Birds*. By the end of this movie, the birds have declared an out-and-out war on all unfeathered folk in a small California town. One family who has been continually harassed by the flying fiends decides to risk leaving home to drive away to safety. Slowly and cautiously, they make the treacherous walk to their car and get in. As they do, the camera pulls back and moviegoers can see that every telephone wire, every branch of every tree is thickly populated with birds. It is all too clear from this "bird's-eye view" of the situation that there is no escape.

To have physically arranged such a shot, calling for thousands of

Live-action location for a wild and crazy scene from It's a Mad, Mad, Mad, Mad World. *(Photo courtesy of Linwood G. Dunn, ASC, President, Film Effects of Hollywood)*

Matte painting to be photographically combined with the scene above. (Photo courtesy of Linwood G. Dunn, ASC, President, Film Effects of Hollywood)

The finished scene! Can you tell where the live action stops and the painting begins? (Photo courtesy of Linwood G. Dunn, ASC, President, Film Effects of Hollywood)

birds, would have been nearly impossible. The answer to the problem was to have a master matte-painting artist create part of the scene as a painting.

First, the painter, Albert Whitlock, made sketches of the way he envisioned the final scene with the bird brigade and the frightened family. Then the live action — the family leaving the house and getting into the car — was filmed by only a small part of the camera's lens. The rest of the lens was covered up by a matte. Since no light could enter the lens to expose the matted-over area of the film, that portion of the film remained unexposed.

After the live action was photographed, this roll of partly exposed film was taken to a matte-painting studio. A small section of test footage was developed and one frame of the live action was then projected onto a canvas so Mr. Whitlock could begin his painting of the bird multitudes.

The actual rendering of a matte painting progresses in much the same way as that of glass painting, except that instead of part of a set being blended into a painting, the small projected image of the live action is used as the starting point of the artwork. The matte painter must continually check to make sure that the painting blends in with the live-action scene. And again, test shots are taken to make sure that the two elements are perfectly matched before the final take.

When Albert Whitlock's painting of the birds was finished, the area where the live-action scene had been projected was painted solid black. This blacked-out part of the canvas did not reflect any light at all into the camera when the matte painting was photographed on the *same* piece of film that contained the live action. The black area, in other words, now acted as a matte and kept the live-action portion of the film from being double exposed.

The on-screen effect of the painting combined with the live action was incredibly real. Yet, oddly enough, the style of the matte painting is not super-realistic. It is actually impressionistic. This is because of the way the eye sees objects. The eye tends to blur together things in the distance. So Albert Whitlock—and other matte artists—slightly blur the backgrounds of matte paintings so that they will look natural to moviegoers.

Since this particular matte painting of the birds was to be on screen for a rather long time, a clever technique was used to add some "movement" to the artwork. Small holes were punched into the matte canvas, and as the scene was filmed, a light was waved around behind the painting. This slight motion of light gave the impression on screen of motion: that a few birds were actually restlessly shifting as they waited for their final attack.

Matte paintings are used extensively in the movies. Usually they provide backgrounds and aren't noticeable because audience attention is focused on the live action. These paintings can be successfully combined with live-action scenes because incredibly steady cameras have been developed. If the camera moved at all, even a fraction of an inch, while it was photographing a painting, the matte lines—or the edges of the pieces of the matte "jigsaw puzzle"—would be off center just slightly and audiences would be able to see a line on screen where the mattes should have blended together perfectly.

Scenes achieved with an *in-camera matte*, like the one just described, give a very high-quality image, since the entire effect is photographed *on one strip of film*. But such mattes are limiting in the same way that glass shots and split-screen shots are limiting: the actors must stay within a certain area. Again, if they move too far in the wrong direction, they will cross a matte line and, on screen, part of them will seem to disappear.

Tricky special-effects experts have, of course, solved this problem by creating a different kind of matte with an amazing machine called an optical printer.

A matte painting of Emerald City from The Wizard of Oz. *The live action of Dorothy and her companions easing down the Yellow Brick Road was matted into the empty pathway in the painting. (MGM, 1939; Museum of Modern Art/Film Stills Archive)*

MEANWHILE, BACK AT THE LAB

So far, all of the optical illusions described in this chapter can be done on a single strip of film — *the original negative.* Even if the strip of film has gone past the camera's lens more than once or has picked up a projected background with live action, it is still the original negative that has captured all of the images for a complete optical effect.

Many optical effects seen on the screen today are not created on the original negative, however. They are made from combining layers of film — and sometimes layers upon layers upon layers of film — together in the same sort of jigsaw-puzzle arrangement that has been described before. The instrument responsible for sandwiching these separate strips into one strip of film is the optical printer.

This amazing maze of machinery is an optical printer belonging to Mr. Linwood Dunn of Film Effects of Hollywood. (Photo courtesy of Linwood G. Dunn, ASC, President, Film Effects of Hollywood)

Very simply, an optical printer houses a movie camera that faces a movie projector. The shutters of the camera and the projector are synchronized so that the split second the projector's shutter opens and projects a frame of film, the camera's shutter opens to photograph that frame.

A positive print of a movie, for example, can be threaded into the projector of an optical printer while a reel of unexposed film, or "raw stock" as it is called, is loaded into an optical printer's camera. Now, if the positive print of the movie is simply run through the projector, the camera can photograph this movie, frame for frame. The exposed film can then be treated to create a *negative print* of the movie. If this negative is processed further, a *positive print* of the movie will result. This print will be an *exact duplicate* of the movie that was threaded into the optical printer's projector. This, in fact, is one function of the optical printer: it makes exact copies of movies.

Now, on to the optical printer's many other talents. If a director, for example, has shot a race car sequence at normal speed and then decides that he wishes he had shot it with fast motion so that it would look a little zippier on the screen, he can go to the optical printer for help. The film of the race scene is threaded into the optical printer's projector and raw stock is loaded into the optical printer's camera. Now a dial on the printer is set so that as the camera photographs the race scene, it will film three frames in a row and then skip one. This skipping of every fourth frame will be repeated over and over again as the whole race scene is filmed and will produce a copy of the scene with fewer frames—25 per cent fewer—than the original scene. When this scene is projected at normal speed, the race scene will look 25 per cent faster than it did before. This new footage can now be spliced into the film to replace the original scene.

To create a kind of slow motion, the optical printer's camera can be set so that it will photograph every third frame of a movie two times—or every second frame three times—depending on how slow the slow motion is supposed to be. The optical printer can't really create *true* slow motion, since it cannot break down already photo-graphed action into any smaller parts, but by repeating existing frames more than once, it will slow down the action of the film on the screen.

The optical printer can do split screens, fades, and dissolves. It can create reverse filming—for scenes like the one in *Superman* when the San Andreas fault is "repaired" by the visitor from Krypton. But the most spectacular function of the optical printer is its ability to layer together different pieces of film.

But before going on to the optical printer's "layering" techniques, it would be a good idea to review the idea of *positive* and *negative*. In the previous chapter it was explained that when light hits unexposed film, it "burns" an image onto the film. When an exposed strip of film is taken to a processing lab, it is first put into a bath of chemicals that turn it into a *negative*. On the negative, everything is just the opposite from the way it is on a positive print; light colors appear to be dark and vice versa. From this negative, it is possible for the film lab to create a *positive print* of the film. They can do this in a number of ways, but no matter how it is done, film always goes from negative to positive when it is being duplicated.

NOW YOU SEE HIM, NOW YOU DON'T

Remember the Invisible Man? The one with the grudge against the world? Before his death scene, he spent most of his time on screen wearing a suit and hat. To hide the fact that his hands were invisible, he wore gloves and he kept his face wrapped in bandages, with breathing space provided by an artificial nose. Such a "visible" Invisible Man was easy to film. So was the completely "invisible" Invisible Man. If he had to lift something and move it around the room in his totally invisible state, the object was simply suspended from fine wires and moved by effects workers in the rafters. But the scenes where the Invisible Man discarded his gloves, unwrapped his bandages, and was seen as an invisible body in a suit of clothes were extremely tricky to film.

The special-effects ace on this picture, John P. Fulton, first tried to solve this problem by suspending an empty suit of clothes from the ceiling on thin wires, but this created a sort of "limp dishrag" effect. So Fulton turned to the optical printer to solve the dilemma. The procedure he used is somewhat complicated, but quite ingenious.

The Invisible Man was filmed in black and white, so Fulton had a totally black set constructed. Its walls and floor were covered with black velvet—the most non-reflective material known—so that no light at all would reflect from the background set into the camera's lens. A stunt man, dressed in a black velvet body suit and tights, black velvet gloves, and a black velvet hood which covered his entire head, was called to the set. When he stood in front of the black velvet background, he became truly invisible—just like the old joke about the polar bear in the snowstorm, only in reverse! The stunt man was then dressed over his velvet costume in whatever clothes were called for in a scene—a suit and hat, for example. These clothes were light-colored to contrast with the dark background. As the stunt man moved against the black background, it did look, through the camera's viewfinder, as if an invisible being was inside the suit of clothes. The only filming problems occurred when the stunt man accidentally put his hand in front of some part of his body. Then the camera

The Invisible Man is caught off guard. Notice the tricky eye-hiding goggles and the phony nose. (Copyright © Universal City Studios, Inc. All rights reserved.)

could clearly see the shape of the black glove on the light suit and the illusion of invisibility was destroyed.

As Fulton photographed the stunt man, only the suit and hat registered on the film. The rest of the set was so dark that it reflected no light into the camera's lens. The areas of the black velvet background and the stunt man's hooded head and gloved hands remained *unexposed* on the film.

Even before Fulton photographed the stunt man, he had filmed, on regular sets, the scenes in which the Invisible Man was to appear. In a living room scene, for example, an actor simply addressed empty space in the room when he was supposed to be talking to the Invisible Man or listened attentively looking into another empty space as the Invisible Man's lines were delivered. When all of the live-action scenes on regular sets were filmed, Fulton had *positive prints* made of them. Then he turned his attention to adding in the Invisible Man.

To do this, Fulton made both a negative and a positive print of the stunt-man-in-the-suit scenes. On the black-and-white negative, the light areas of the suit became totally black. The areas of the negative which had never been exposed to light — the black velvet background as well as the hood and gloves — became completely clear on the negative. So, this negative simply had a black silhouette of a suit printed on each frame.

Fulton next took the *positive print* of a scene shot on the regular set — the living room scene, for example — and the *negative print* of the corresponding suit scene and threaded the two layers of film into the optical printer's projector. Then, with raw film in the optical printer's camera. Fulton photographed the living room scene with the "suit" negative in front of it. Naturally, this dark silhouette of the suit acted as a matte. In each frame of film, it kept light from going through and exposing the film in just the area of the suit. Since the suit changed positions from frame to frame, we say that it "traveled" and acted as a *traveling matte*.

The result of this procedure was a strip of film showing the living room scene with a completely transparent "hole" in the shape of a suit in each frame. This film was then rewound inside the optical printer's camera. Now the *positive print* of the suit scene was put into the optical printer's projector and it was printed onto this same strip of film — exactly "filling in" the hole left by the suit matte. The end result of this intricate process was a perfect layering of these pieces of film to make one remarkable scene!

COLOR COORDINATION

The black velvet backgrounds worked fine for black-and-white films, but they won't do for color films. There is a process that serves the same function, however, called the *blue-screen process*. Very simply (for the technique is quite complex) the color *blue* is screened out by a certain photographic process. When a person stands in front of a bright blue screen and is photographed, the result is a strip of film in which only the person appears. The background is totally clear. (When *Superman* was filmed, the blue-screen process was used in many scenes and the moviemakers had to be careful to select a color for Superman's tights and costume that would not be filtered out when he was filmed in front of a blue screen.)

With the blue-screen process, a film maker can use the same sort of traveling matte system that was used in *The Invisible Man:* an actor or a spaceship or any other element photographed in front of a blue screen can — through photographic processing — become its own matte. The blue-screen system allows a film maker to create separate strips of film with just a single element of a scene on each strip. With the help of the optical printer, each of the separate elements can be combined onto one piece of film — with everything on it.

A movie that took full advantage of blue screen — as well as just about every other special-effects trick in the book — was *Star Wars* (1977), the space opera about a young hero, Luke Skywalker, who becomes involved in fantastic intergalactic adventures. With the aid of his friends, Luke fights the forces of evil, lead by the hulking Darth Vader. At the end of the film, the forces of good gather to wage war on the forces of evil. Luke and company pilot planes known as X-wing fighters. The bad guys are in Imperial T.I.E. fighters. Before long, a good old–fashioned air battle is underway with the planes firing laser beams at each other. Hit planes spin out of control and crash or blow apart in violent explosions. At last, the good guys score a direct hit and Vader's capital of evil, the Death Star, explodes with a fiery bang.

This climactic sequence could never have been filmed without the blue-screen process — or without the imaginative vision of the film's originator and director, George Lucas. Lucas had always been a fan of old World War II movies, where American Mustang planes battled Japanese Zeros in plane-to-plane combat. When he conceived the idea of an aerial battle scene, he knew where to go for research. Lucas collected lots of these World War II movies and, with his creative film crew, he watched them again and again. He noticed every little detail: how the Mustangs tilted as they were being chased by the Zeros; how the Zeros looked as they spun out of control and dove to the earth below; how the gunfire looked when it made a direct hit and how it looked when it missed.

Lucas then had the parts of his favorite dogfight sequences translated onto a *storyboard*. A storyboard is a series of drawings by an artist that shows how each shot in a movie will look. It gives the position of the camera and depicts where each element in the scene will be. On the *Star Wars* storyboard, some interesting changes took place. The American Mustangs were turned into good-guy X-wing fighters. The Zeros became the Imperial T.I.E. fighters. The daylight sky became star-filled "deep space"; bullets fired became laser beams; and the earth's horizon below became the surface of the Death Star planet.

After each scene was planned in detail, the shooting of the fight sequence began. The X-wings and T.I.E. fighters were miniatures— about the size of an average plane from a model kit—but they were photographed to look the size of actual fighter planes. Each segment of the dogfight sequence was photographed more or less in this way: An X-wing fighter was mounted on a long arm—called a "pylon" —in front of a blue screen. The pylon was wrapped in blue material so that it would blend in with the blue screen and not show up on any of the film. The X-wing was photographed against the blue-screen background by a very special computer-linked camera. The camera had been programmed with information on exactly how to photograph this plane; exactly what kinds of tilts, rolls, turns, or other maneuvers were called for. But when the shooting began, the plane didn't move a single centimeter. It was the *camera* that did all of the tilting and panning by moving down a long track that was especially built for it. The camera made what were called "passes" at the plane.

After several takes, the X-wing was removed from the pylon and the T.I.E. fighter was mounted in its place. Now, because this incredible camera was hooked up to a computer, it could "remember" the shot it had just made of the X-wing and it shot the scenes of the T.I.E. fighter in *relation* to the earlier shots it had made. After the planes were filmed, the surface of the Death Star was filmed against a blue screen. Each element in the scene was shot in this way, on its own individual strip of film. It was the optical printer that put together this complex jigsaw puzzle. By the time the laser beams, their reflections on the planes, and all necessary shadows were added, as many as 38 layers of film were combined onto one piece of film to create this spectacular scene.

This kind of duplication and fitting together of different parts of a scene represents optical effects at its most complex. It is unbelievably difficult to run so many pieces of film through the printer and have everything match up perfectly. In the shooting of *Star Wars*, the Force that was with the film makers was most likely the optical printer.

OPTICAL CONCLUSIONS

It's safe to say that just about every movie today has some kind of optical effect in it. It may only be the titles, superimposed over the opening scenes in the film by the optical printer. Then again, there are movies that are almost one long optical effect. *Star Wars*, for example, contains 360 separate optical-effects shots. It took an army of 75 skilled effects workers to create all of this trickery, which is on the screen for fully half of the running time of the picture. A movie like this really *is* an optical illusion.

4

Mountains from Molehills:
Miniatures

"You will have the tallest leading man in Hollywood," movie producer Merian C. Cooper promised actress Fay Wray in 1932 when he picked her to star in his latest adventure film. Fay Wray imagined herself playing opposite the top screen idol of the day, Clark Gable, and she almost backed out of the picture when she learned that her costar was to be a thirty-foot ape — King Kong! And if that wasn't disappointing enough, it was only on the screen that Kong looked tall. Fay Wray's leading man was, in reality, only eighteen inches high.

Yes, the hard truth is that the "Eighth Wonder of the World" was not a colossus at all. King Kong was a miniature.

A *miniature* is a small-sized model, built, operated, and photographed so that it will look much larger on screen. Miniatures "double" for burning buildings, sinking ocean liners, crashing cars, and hulking thirty-foot apes. If miniatures are made well and handled skillfully, they can fool audiences into believing that they are the real thing.

Kong, for example, was so realistic, so believable, that it was difficult to convince people that he *was* a miniature. It was a great tribute to Kong's creators that a *Time* magazine writer reported in 1933: "Kong is actually 50' tall, 36' around the chest. His face is 6½' wide

Animator Buz Gibson positions the miniature Kong on a ladder of dowels that becomes the side of the Empire State Building in a finished shot in King Kong, *1933. (The Collection of Orville Goldner)*

with 10-in. teeth and ears 1 ft. long. He has a rubber nose, glass eyes as big as tennis balls."

Actually, the eighteen-inch Kong had a small metal skeleton called an *armature*. This armature had real "ball-and-socket" joints, modeled after the way our own bones are connected. These joints made it possible for Kong to move in a very smooth, lifelike way. On top of this skeleton, flexible muscles of solid rubber were fitted. Then the outer Kong was covered with a coat, not of bear skins, but of pruned rabbit fur. Kong's face was made from rubber and could show several expressions.

Why was a miniature ape used? Well, since there was no chance of a thirty-foot ape answering a casting call for the part of Kong, the only choice was to come up with an ape-substitute. Building a believable thirty-foot mechanical monkey that could stomp down the streets of New York, climb the Empire State Building, and give a convincing acting performance seemed next to impossible. And even if such a beast *could* have been built, the movie producers would have had to ask the key question: *How much would it cost?* A big ape, of course, would cost big money. When building a full-sized mechanical model is too expensive, moviemakers often turn to miniatures. Because they are comparatively easy on the budget, miniatures have become a staple of special-effects work.

But cost is only one reason that miniatures are used in movie making. Safety is another factor. What actor would have taken a role in *The Towering Inferno* if the movie had been shot in an actual skyscraper with a real fire raging out of control? What camera crew would have agreed to shoot *The Poseidon Adventure* if part of the job had involved being aboard an actual ocean liner that capizes? In these disaster movies, miniatures of the flaming building and the sinking ship were used to film scenes that would have been terribly dangerous and nearly impossible to shoot in life-size reality.

SNEAKY TRICKS DEPARTMENT

The crucial thing in filming miniatures is to make them look real. There are few things more disappointing than being totally involved in a sci-fi movie, for example, and suddenly seeing an obviously toy-size spaceship wobble across the screen on a visible wire. The scene is lost; the illusion of the film is shattered. Fortunately, miniature-model makers know a few tricks that help to make their models look believable.

Miniatures are sometimes classified into two groups: *still miniatures* and *moving miniatures*. Since very few things that we see in the real world are actually completely motionless—a breeze flutters the leaves in a tree, a light blinks on in a house at night, a bird flits by a telephone pole—a miniature that moves even slightly will give a more lifelike impression on the screen than a still one.

Effects experts Cedric Gibbons and A. Arnold Gillespie knew this when they worked on the silent version of *Ben Hur* (1925). They needed to build a set of the Circus Maximus, the huge stadium where chariot races were held in ancient Rome. They constructed a full-size set for part of the Circus Maximus. This was where the live action—the actual chariot race—was to take place. But it would have been far too costly to build a full-size replica of the entire stadium.

The solution was to create the rest of the set in miniature. This

The famous chariot race from the 1926 silent version of Ben Hur *combined foreground live action with an extraordinary miniature set. (1925, MGM; Museum of Modern Art/Film Stills Archive)*

miniature part showed thousands of spectators in the far galleries, supposedly watching the races. The camera was placed in such a way that, when photographed, the miniature blended in with the life-size set. (This shot was set up something like a glass shot.) But Gibbons and Gillespie realized that if the camera focused on the tiny set for any length of time, audiences would notice that the people in the galleries never moved and the set would be given away as a miniature. So, in a stroke of genius, they built in several sections of tiny seats with ten thousand miniature people in them who, triggered by a mechanical device, could all stand up and cheer!

The size of miniatures is another important factor that model makers need to consider. In general, the bigger a miniature is, the more realistic it will look on the screen. Tiny miniatures are fine for long shots, but miniatures that are used for close-ups are usually built to as big a scale as the budget will allow. And many times it is actually less expensive to build large miniatures. The amount of money that is spent on extra materials for large miniatures is often less than the money needed to pay for the extra time and labor to do the intricate detail work on smaller models.

Occasionally, miniatures reach such proportions that the name "miniature" no longer fits. The makers of *Earthquake* needed a miniature to represent the Hollywood Dam, which bursts in the climactic scene of the film. The actual dam is 880 feet across. It was decided that, in order for it to look good on the screen, the miniature could be no less than *sixteen times smaller* than the real dam — but that's still 54 feet across! Each part of the miniature dam had to be sixteen times smaller than the equivalent part of the real dam. Since *one* foot of the miniature dam represented *sixteen* feet of the real dam, we say that the miniature was built on a *scale* of 1 foot to 16 feet or *1:16*.

Miniatures can be built to all sorts of scales. The Death Star in *Star Wars*, for example, had a diameter of only a couple of feet, although it was supposed to represent an orb that was a mile in diameter. It was built on a scale of 1:2,400. The Death Star worked at this minute scale because it had an incredible amount of detail on it. The camera could get very close to it to make audiences think they were looking at something much more enormous. But most miniatures, particularly those representing familar objects such as cars, buildings, planes, and so on, must be built on a scale of at least 1:24. If

Miniature houses were swept away when a 54-foot "miniature" replica of the Hollywood Dam burst in Earthquake. *(Copyright © Universal City Studios, Inc. All rights reserved.)*

they are built on a smaller scale, they will look like miniatures on the screen.

Distance and perspective must also be taken into account in constructing miniatures. Look out a window and you will notice that objects closest to you look the largest while those far away appear to be very small; a car right outside the window will look its actual size while an apartment building in the distance may seem very tiny. You know that the apartment building is really much bigger than the car, but because it is far away, it looks smaller. *The farther away something is, the smaller it seems to be.*

For *Close Encounters of the Third Kind*, film makers searched for a panoramic view of Indiana countryside to show in a wide-angle shot. They were unable to find one that exactly suited their needs, so they decided to build the landscape in miniature. Yet even a miniature set of the countryside would end up being huge if the houses farthest from the camera were to look small enough and appear to be in proper perspective. To save themselves the task of building such a mammoth set, model makers created the *illusion* of distance. The miniature houses closest to the camera were built on a fairly large scale. Houses, barns, fences, trees, and so on that were to be placed farther and farther from the camera were built on smaller and smaller scales, tapering down to houses no bigger than a dime! This trick, known as *mixed-scale sets*, lets film makers create, in small spaces, miniature sets that are supposed to span great distances.

If you look at a car close to you, you may notice that you can see such things as hubcaps, hood ornaments, and even small dents. But if you look at a car that is a few streets away, you may only be able to tell that it is a blue car. The amount of *detail* that you can see decreases as things get farther away from you.

When model makers create sets, they must add lots of detail to buildings, cars, or whatever will be close to the camera. They may even wish to scuff up such miniatures to have them show everyday wear and tear so that they won't look like models, brand new out of the mold. For buildings farther from the camera, less detail is added. In fact, if houses far from the camera show up on the screen with too much detail, it will give the set away as a miniature every time.

PINT-SIZED PROBLEMS

Model makers can create miniature spaceships and miniature planets; they can make believable miniature fighter planes and battleships; they can fashion miniature apes and dinosaurs. Is there anything that is impossible to miniaturize? Yes . . . *water.*

Water can dampen the spirits of any film maker trying to photograph it in a miniature setting. A saying in the business goes, "You can't make small water!" No matter what size container it is in, water acts in roughly the same way. The behavior of waves, the distance between them, or the size of a drop of water simply cannot be made smaller. If a tiny miniature ship is set afloat in water with any waves at all, it will bob about like a bathtub toy. For this reason, miniatures that are going to be photographed in water are usually built to as large a scale as possible and are weighted down so that they are heavy enough to ride the waves realistically. Scales for miniature ships range from 1:24 to 1:4. At an average scale of 1:16, a 640-foot battleship, such as the one depicted in *Tora! Tora! Tora!* (1970), became a "miniature" 40 feet long!

Since these miniatures are so large, the places where they are filmed also need to be big. Some sea scenes are actually filmed in the ocean, but conditions are more easily controlled in the movie studios' large, outdoor tanks. It is not unusual for such tanks to have a surface area of ninety thousand square feet! Since effects people must spend a great deal of time wading in the tanks setting up the shots, the tanks are only about three feet deep. A forty-foot ocean liner would have trouble sinking — if that's what the script called for — in three feet of water, so there are also special areas called "wells" which are twelve to fifteen feet deep. To make sure that the tank's shallow areas aren't visible, blue dye is often added to the water to conceal the bottom and any equipment or cables used to propel the miniature ships.

Any weather conditions a scriptwriter can come up with — from gentle sea breezes to hurricanes and tidal waves — can be simulated in the studio tanks. Stormy weather is created with the help of giant fans and "wave machines," which can stir up the water to a frantic pitch. But if the waves splashed against the back of the tank, audiences would see that the scene was not really taking place on the "open seas," so a continuous stream of water is pumped through the tank and allowed to flow over a spillway or lowered area at the back end of the tank. This causes the waves to subside and fall down the spillway. The camera is placed on the opposite side of the tank, just above the water level, as though looking up at the ships, which makes them look larger. The spillway then makes a nice straight edge of water which blends against the sky for a realistic horizon line.

Although water cannot be miniaturized, there are a couple of things that special-effects men can do to make it behave the way they want it to. One way to make slightly smaller water droplets and waves is to reduce the surface tension of the water by adding a "wetting agent" such as Lestoil. To make small whitecaps appear on waves, a bit of detergent can be added to the water. Great care has to be taken, however, not to overdo this technique, or instead of a stormy sea, the tank will become a giant bubble bath!

Because water is so difficult to work with, sometimes substitutes for it are used in miniature sets. Have you ever seen a long shot of a waterfall with a fantastic white spray? Chances are that it may not have been a waterfall at all, but a man-made fall created by pouring marble dust down a miniature cliff. Flour is sometimes added to the marble dust to give it even more "spray." For a distant river, where real water would trickle by too quickly, thicker substances, such as Karo syrup, may be added to the water. Faraway lakes are sometimes faked by laying hundreds of cellophane strips in the same direction over a blue board. A fan blown gently on the strips will give the impression of shimmering water.

Like water, fire is difficult to miniaturize. Yet many fire effects are done in miniature because it is so much safer and less costly than creating a life-size blaze. The size of miniature flames can be regulated somewhat by using gas jets — similar to the flame controls on a gas stove. To keep flames from devouring a miniature building in a split second, a fire effect may be extended by coating the set with paraffin, which burns quite slowly.

Miniatures that are to be destroyed by flame are built to as large a scale as possible so that the fire will look correct in proportion. In *The Towering Inferno*, for example, the miniature for the 138-story building was 9 stories high. If a small-scale set must be used for some reason, effects teams can create a realistic fire scene with the aid of *distance*. That is, they can place a row of miniature houses — or housefronts only — facing the camera and then position a row of flames far enough *behind* the miniature set so that the two elements appear to match in scale when viewed through the camera lens. Although actually many feet away from the set, the flames will seem to be leaping from the rooftops and lapping through the windows for a scaled-down "three-alarmer."

Miniature explosions must be carefully planned so that they will happen dramatically on screen — and safely off screen. For *Air Mail* (1932), effects expert John Fulton built two planes that were required by the script to have a midair collision. Fulton made the two miniature planes out of soft balsa wood so that they would smash easily.

When the planes were completed, Fulton broke their wings in exactly the places he wanted them to break during the crash. Then he glued them ever so lightly back together again, making sure that they would rebreak on the slightest impact. To make the collision even more spectacular, Fulton loaded small flash-powder bombs into the planes. As the cameras rolled, the planes zoomed toward each other and collided with a fiery bang. Fulton's well-planned explosion was a smashing success.

The explosions of the miniature X-wing and T.I.E. fighters in the dogfight scenes from *Star Wars* were done in much the same way. The models were pre-broken, lightly reglued, and then hung by thin blue wires in front of a blue screen. Off to the side of the screen was a fan. As the planes exploded, the fan blew sparks and debris past the camera's lens so that it looked like the exploding planes were moving forward.

The main problem with making miniature explosions look real on the screen is that they have to be *exactly* the right size to match up with the object being exploded. A miniature plane zapped by a huge blast will look like a toy being blown up, while an explosion that is just slightly too small will seem like a disappointing fizzle.

Another vexing problem faced by model makers is how to miniaturize people. Since everyone knows so well what people look like, it is very hard to fool an audience with a miniature person. For this reason, miniature people are used mainly for very brief long-shots. In *The Wizard of Oz*, a small replica of the Wicked Witch (Margaret Hamilton) was used in distant scenes of her flying away on her broomstick. The miniature Kong held an even tinier Fay Wray doll in his fist, but the camera focused on it so fleetingly that it was difficult even for Fay Wray to tell whether it was a shot of her or her diminutive stand-in.

A scene from the comedy caper *It's a Mad, Mad, Mad, Mad World* (1963), which is about a wild search for buried treasure, gives some idea of the lengths to which special-effects people will go in order to get a realistic shot of miniature people. The scene shows several of the movie's characters hanging on for dear life to a fire escape that has broken loose from a building. As the people attempt to climb onto an extended fire-engine ladder that has been raised to them, suddenly the ladder begins to swing madly back and forth, catapulting people every which way.

Effects experts perfect details on miniature people for It's a Mad, Mad, Mad, Mad World. *(Photo courtesy of Linwood G. Dunn, ASC, President, Film Effects of Hollywood)*

Close-ups of the people were done with the real actors. Miniature doubles, built on a scale of 1:6, were used to show the ladder bouncing on to live power lines and spilling people into them. Another set of miniatures, this time on a 1:12 scale, was used for long shots and animated sequences, while still another small-fry set of miniatures, only 1:48 in scale, was filmed in the extreme long shots. Skillful cutting from the live actors to the three "casts" of scaled-down replicas in this hilarious scene gave audiences no time to think about spotting miniature people.

Everyday objects—cars, trucks, bicycles, and the like—are also

Close-up of the miniature people built on a scale where 1 inch represented 1 foot, or a scale of 1:12. (Photo courtesy of Linwood G. Dunn, ASC, President, Film Effects of Hollywood)

tricky to miniaturize. We are familiar with these things, and so we notice if a car's tires are too thick for its body or if the handle on a truck door is too small. Such common objects must be crafted with special care in order to fool us.

Scenes like this one, with live actors and stunt men, were intercut with the miniatures to give the scene a real feeling. (© 1963, United Artists)

Sci-fi miniatures, on the other hand — UFOs, spaceships, robots, and the like — have this advantage: no one is sure what they are *supposed* to look like. There is no real-life model against which to compare the miniatures for detail and accuracy. Still, audiences are sophisticated enough to know that most space conveyances probably *are* miniatures, and so they must be convinced that the vehicles are "real."

Steven Spielberg, director of *Close Encounters of the Third Kind*, read all he could about UFO sightings before making his film. He paid particular attention to the way people described the UFOs they had seen. Most of them did not describe the UFOs as being a particular shape or size or made of any particular material. What they did emphasize was a quality of bright light shining from them. So, this was what Spielberg wanted, and it was up to special-effects man Douglas Trumbull to achieve it.

Trumbull filmed each UFO separately with miniature lights exposed by several "passes" of the camera to get multiple-exposed, overlapping lights effect. But the first such shots of the UFOs were disappointing. Trumbull wanted more of a glow from the UFOs. He knew that when a bright light—such as a landing light from a plane, shines down from the night sky, a beam of light is visible. The brilliant light seems to "spread out" through the atmosphere, creating a kind of soft haze. It was this haze or glow that Trumbull was after. But when he photographed the miniature lights, on a 1:20 scale, the result was merely pinpoints of light. The miniature lights were too small to create a "spreading out" effect in the air. Then Trumbull hit upon an ingenious solution to the no-glow problem. Since the miniature UFOs were built on a 1:20 scale, Trumbull brought smoke machines to the set and filled the air with a smoky haze until it was exactly 20 times dirtier than normal air! With an atmosphere this "thick," the tiny lights gave off just the right halo-glow!

Filming in this smoke-filled environment was no picnic. The film crew had to don gas masks to protect themselves from the oil-based smoke and the camera operators spent hours cleaning the smog out of their lenses. But the final effect of those shimmering UFOs was worth all of the dirty work.

Early sci-fi films rarely showed this much concern for "realism." The Buck Rogers serials of the early 1930s were full of rocket ships that jerked across a cardboard sky. Smoke from the rocket engines floated up while sparks fell heavily to the ground—dead giveaways that these airships were not in gravity-less outer space.

A brightly lit spaceship comes closer and closer in Close Encounters of the Third Kind. *(Copyright © 1978 Columbia Pictures Industries, Inc.)*

The camera can do quite a bit to help miniatures pass for the real McCoy. It is usually positioned directly in front of a miniature—as high as the eye level of a person the same scale as the miniature set would be. Camera operators keep their cameras focused on a miniature for no more than a couple of seconds. This way the audience does not have time to spot the miniature for what it is. Scenes with miniatures usually involve a lot of quick cutting back and forth from the miniatures to the live action. The least noticeable of all is a miniature that has been combined—by split screen or blue screen or some other optical process—in the same shot with live actors. If the action is fast-paced, no one will notice that the home being demolished by a giant wave is really no bigger than a dollhouse.

HIGH SPEED AHEAD

In many a low-budget sci-fi flick, travelers somehow end up in a land where prehistoric beasts still roam. If these dinosaurs look startlingly like large lizards it may be because these "roles" often go to actual lizards, which have extra horns and spikes glued to their bodies to make them look more primitive and terrifying. And, not so surprisingly, the lizards aren't large at all. They only look that way because they are placed in miniature sets with tiny trees, rocks, lakes, and bushes. Photographed at close range, the lizards appear to be towering beasts, smashing tall trees and wreaking havoc with every step. The only problem with this setup is that prehistoric beasts, as we know from their skeletons, were immense creatures. They moved slowly and ponderously through the primeval forests. But the lizard actors scamper about quickly and can easily destroy a scene's illusion. Film makers solve this problem with their cameras. Instead of filming a little lizard at the normal camera speed of 24 frames per second (24 fps), they use the technique of high-speed filming. They might film at four times faster than normal speed, or 96 fps. Yet when the film shot at 96 fps is projected at the normal speed in the theater, the effect is not seen as slow motion. The lizard's movements will appear to be four times slower than they actually were, but it will appear to the audience as the right speed for a dinosaur lumbering through the forest.

This technique, called *high-speed filming*, is used to make us think we are seeing *normal* movement rather than slow movement. The speed at which a miniature is photographed is determined by its *scale*. In general, the smaller the scale of the miniature, the faster the camera will have to run to make it look real.

Imagine, for example, that a movie scene calls for an expensive car to spin out of control and go flying off a cliff. Let's say that the real car is 10 feet long and the cliff is 150 feet high. It would take this car about 3 seconds to reach the bottom of the cliff. But just as this real (and expensive) car is about to plummet over the edge of the cliff, a film maker would probably decide to cut to a miniature car in a long shot. If constructed on a scale of 1:10, the miniature car would be 1 foot long and the miniature set would have a cliff 15 feet high. The camera would be placed at the proper angle and the set would be realistically lighted and everything would look perfectly believable — until the miniature car went off the cliff. The miniature would fall through space much too quickly to be in keeping with its scale. Because of the effect of gravity — a falling object picks up speed as it falls — the miniature car would reach the bottom of the 15-foot cliff in less than 1 second, while an actual 3,000-pound car would fall from a 150-foot cliff in about 3 seconds.

People are constantly observing the way things operate in the real world and audiences would know something was wrong if they were watching a film and saw a car drop from a "150-foot cliff" in less than 1 second. So, it's high-speed filming to the rescue! If the miniature fall took 1 second and it needs to last 3 seconds on screen, then the cameras must shoot the scene at *three times* the normal camera speed, or at 72 fps . . . just what the expensive full-scale fall would have taken.

It's also high-speed filming that is responsible for so many of Godzilla's rampages. Godzilla, the 400-foot monster from Japan, awakened by an atomic explosion, spends most of its on-screen time stomping on everything in sight. Although Godzilla isn't a model — it's played by a man in a monster suit — it is a miniature, since a man is standing in for a 400-foot monster. Godzilla tramples miniature sets that come about up to his knees. Using high-speed filming to make Godzilla's rampages look believable, Toho studios in Japan quickly and cheaply produced one Godzilla movie after another. (It is an interesting side note that one movie, *King Kong versus Godzilla* (1963), also had Kong played by an actor in a monster suit. In the

Japanese version of the movie, Godzilla won the final battle, but in the film released in the United States, Kong was the champ!)

The miniature explosions of the planes in *Star Wars* were filmed at 100 to 150 fps. Slowing down the on-screen speed of the explosions made them look much more sensational, the Death Star extravaganza explosion at the end was shot at the incredibly high speed of 300 fps!

MORE MONKEY BUSINESS

As you know, Kong was not played by a man in a monkey suit in the 1933 version of *King Kong*. Actually, he was played not by one but by *six* identical 18-inch apes. The process that made the miniature apes come "alive," according to *The Making of King Kong*, worked this way.

Miniature jungle sets were built on waist-high tabletops so that the people who moved Kong, the *animators*, could reach him conveniently. Tiny holes were drilled into the soft pine tabletop at close, regular intervals. This way, special "clamps" could be attached to Kong's feet and put through the holes in each table to hold the miniature steady as it "walked." The holes in the tables could not be seen by the camera's eye because they were covered over with "jungle foliage" — twigs and small seedling plants.

Kong's creator, Willis O'Brien, and his crew of animators watched many slow-motion films of actual animals walking, running, leaping, and moving in all sorts of ways before they began their animation.

Then Kong was positioned carefully in the miniature jungle setting. A camera was placed at a low angle in front of the set. Now a single frame of film was exposed. Then Kong's position was changed ever so slightly, and another frame of film was exposed. This process continued over and over and over again, one frame at a time, capturing on film each slight change in Kong's position. Little by little his arm would stretch up to swat at a miniature creature flying above him or his head would gradually turn to the side. The changes in the model's position from frame to frame had to be very minor or else the on-screen motions would appear to be jerky. To call this procedure time-consuming is putting it mildly. Twenty-four individual frames had to be shot with Kong in a slightly different position each time before *one second* of screen action was obtained!

At last, after a whole scene had been shot — which sometimes took an entire day and far into the night — the film was developed. Each frame became a tiny still picture. When these photographs were projected onto the movie screen at the normal rate of 24 frames per second, viewers' eyes blended them together and Kong appeared to be stomping through the jungle or fighting a prehistoric reptile.

It's easy to see why this process, known as *three-dimensional (or 3-D) animation*, required six little Kongs; this way several scenes could be photographed at the same time.

Among special-effects people, the undisputed king of 3-D animators is Ray Harryhausen, who has made over a dozen feature-length films such as *The Beast from 20,000 Fathoms* (1953) and *Jason and the Argonauts* (1963) using this frame-by-frame filming technique, which he calls Dynamation.

Harryhausen films are known for their splashy effects. For filming many scenes that combine fantastical miniature creatures — Cyclopes, two-headed birds, and the like — with human actors, he has used a special technique called *miniature rear-screen projection* — guaranteed to cut any hero down to size.

In *The Seventh Voyage of Sinbad* (1958), one scene called for the adventurous hero to have a sword fight with a skeleton. When the time came for Kerwin Mathews, who played Sinbad in the film, to do battle with the bag of bones, Harryhausen gave him detailed scene sketches to study so that he would know exactly how the entire sequence was to be shot. The fight was pre-planned and choreographed with Mathews rehearsing each part of it with an Olympic fencing master. Then, when he was ready to do a real "take," the fencing master stepped off of the set and the cameras rolled away at Mathews, stabbing and slashing at thin air. Mathews had to remember *exactly* when each stab of the sword had to be made and also had to stop his sword at times quite suddenly, as though he had hit the blade of his invisible opponent's sword. This "simple" sword-fight scene required twenty-four consecutive hours of filming before it was considered perfect.

This furious fight footage was developed and carefully edited to select the best shots in the scene. It was then threaded into a rear

Thanks to effects expert Ray Harryhausen's special animation technique, Dynamation, and thanks to miniature rear projection, actor Kerwin Mathews was able to go one on one with a skeleton in The Seventh Voyage of Sinbad. *(© 1958, Columbia Pictures)*

projector. This projector was aimed at the back of the rear-projection screen—a miniature one—that had been carefully camouflaged in a miniature setting. The first frame of Mathews' sword fight was projected through the rear screen and it showed up on the front of the screen, like a tiny slide. Then the skeleton—which was really only eight inches high—was positioned by an animator in relation to the screen so that, through the camera's lens, it looked as if the skeleton were in a fighting stance opposite Mathews.

With the skeleton in position, the animator stepped out of the way. The camera in front of the skeleton and screen clicked, and *one* frame

*An angry two-headed bird menaces Sinbad's crew after they have killed its
young in* The Seventh Voyage of Sinbad. *Again, rear projection is
responsible for the apparent size of this monster. (© 1958, Columbia Pictures)*

of film was shot. Then the projector operator projected the next
frame of Mathews through the tiny rear-projection screen. The
animator stepped back into the miniature set and moved the skeleton
a fraction of an inch to fit with Mathews' slightly changed position.
After the animator stepped out of the set again, another frame of film
was exposed. This laborious process continued, over and over and
over again, thousands of times, to film one of the world's longest
animated fight scenes.

   Most of Harryhausen's films require actors to do scenes "solo" and then miniature monsters—who sometimes appear to tower over the rear-projected heroes—are added later. "Fortunately," says Harryhausen, "most actors have such lively imaginations that they actually like to play scenes to a wall!" To help these actors out, Harryhausen will sometimes provide a cardboard cutout the size and shape that the monster will be in the film. This cutout is used in rehearsals so that the actor can get a clear picture of just what it is he's up against. During the "takes," Harryhausen may have an assistant place a long and very, very thin pole in front of the actor, just where the monster will be added later on. This pole has marks where a creature's head, eyes, arms, and other features will be. Affectionately known as "the monster stick," the pole gives the actor something *real* to focus on in a scene. Later, when the scene is projected onto the miniature projection screen and the monster stick is visible, the animator cleverly hides it from the camera's view by placing the miniature monster directly in front of it.

SMALL CHANGE

The 3-D animation process is about as time-consuming as any activity can be. It is also costly, requiring many pieces of expensive optical equipment to produce really first-class results. Yet, it is the only way known to get an effect that both looks real and yet seems fascinatingly unreal too. Luckily for audiences who thrive on fantasy, there are still a few film makers willing to take all the time and trouble to bring miniature creatures "to life" in the same way that the eighteen-inch King Kong was animated way back in 1933.

5

Mechanical Monsters: Full-Scale Effects

At the end of *The Wizard of Oz*, the Wicked Witch of the West has finally captured Dorothy and friends. Gleefully, the Witch sets fire to the Scarecrow. In an attempt to save her friend, Dorothy picks up a bucket of water and heaves it at him. Much of the water accidentally splashes on the Wicked Witch and, emitting a stream of shrieks and curses, the Witch begins melting . . . melting . . . melting . . . until there is nothing left of her but an empty cloak and hat. Dorothy has saved the day — thanks to *mechanical special effects*.

For this "melting" effect, Margaret Hamilton, who portrayed the evil witch, stood on a small elevator platform built into the floor of the studio. The hem of her full-length witch's cloak was nailed to the floor of the set around the platform. When Judy Garland, who played Dorothy, threw the bucket of water on the witch, the elevator platform began descending below the floor, until it lowered nearly six feet and Margaret Hamilton had completely disappeared, leaving only her clothes in a steamy pile. (Steam was provided courtesy of dry ice hidden in the hem of her cloak.)

The small elevator that enabled Margaret Hamilton to disappear qualifies as a mechanical effect. Mechanical effects in the movies are offshoots of physical effects, such as trapdoors, revolving platforms,

The Wicked Witch of the West, played by Margaret Hamilton, is "liqui-dated" in The Wizard of Oz. *(Copyright © 1939, MGM; Museum of Modern Art/Film Stills Archive)*

and support wires, that have been used on the live stage for years. Anything that is made to move by machinery can be considered a mechanical effect, so that term is really a catchall phrase for many different kinds of trickery. In this chapter on full-scale mechanical effects, secrets will be revealed about the different ways used by effects experts to get things moving in the movies.

A MONSTER WITH PLENTY OF PULL

In 1912, Méliès made a film called *Conquest of the Pole* which showed an unlucky explorer being devoured by a huge Frost Giant.

Méliès' Frost Giant traps unlucky Arctic explorers in Conquest of the Pole. *(Museum of Modern Art/Film Stills Archive)*

This giant, who popped out from the Arctic ice, was 20 feet tall from the waist up. He was constructed from a wooden skeleton covered over with cardboard and plaster, and was able to move his arms, eyes, and man-eating mouth. The secret behind the Frost Giant's movements was a corps of men inside him who operated a system of *pulleys*.

A pulley is just a wheel with a rope threaded over it. When you raise a flag on a flagpole, you are using a simple pulley. The advantage of using pulleys rather than merely tying a rope directly to the Frost Giant's arm, for example, is that several pulleys can be hooked up together and the rope running through the wheels may be pulled in the easiest direction from the most convenient operating position. Pulleys, however, cannot make a heavy load any easier to lift and so they are used today only if an effect involves moving something quite light and usually not very complicated.

This Frost Giant, by the way, is an example of what mechanical effects workers call an *action prop*. An action prop is basically any prop that is built to move. Action props often stand in for animals that would be difficult to work with on a movie set—a giant turtle, for example, that might not respond to a director's call for "Action!" Several action prop "feathered fiends" were made for Hitchcock's *The Birds*. In one scene, a crow was to be shown attacking an actor's hand and getting its feathers seriously ruffled in the process. Since there are animal protection laws that prohibit using real animals in scenes where they might be hurt, an action prop had to double for the real bird. Moray eels, snakes, and other animals that are dangerous to work with are also frequently portrayed by action props, as are sea monsters, Frost Giants, and other out-of-this-world creatures that don't really exist.

WIRE WORKS

Another way to get things moving on a movie set is by using piano wire. That's right—the wire inside a piano that is plunked when the keys are hit. Piano wire comes in various thicknesses: for the low notes it's about the width of pencil lead, but for the highest notes, it's not much thicker than a strand of human hair. Yet even the thinnest piano wire is extremely strong, and it's these two qualities—thinness and strength—that make piano wire one of the most important tools of the special-effects trade.

In *Destination Moon* (1950), a science fiction movie that, for its time, was very scientifically accurate, one scene shows an astronaut drifting away in space and being rescued by a fellow astronaut. To give the effect of gravity-less outer space, mechanical-effects experts suspended each of these "astronauts" from the rafters on thirty-six separate strands of wire, and then moved them around like human marionettes. Naturally, the wire had to be thick enough to support the actors safely while being thin enough *not* to show up on camera. To make sure that the wires were hidden from view, one effects worker was kept busy touching up the wires to match the background with a long pole that had a paint-soaked sponge on top. If so much as one wire showed up on the screen when the "rushes"—the film segments shot on the previous day—were viewed, the entire scene had to be reshot.

Wire-hiding is almost always a headache for mechanical-effects teams. Vertically striped wallpaper or anything in the background that can disguise the wires is a help. In the fantasy *Fantastic Voyage* (1966), a miniaturized medical team is injected into the bloodstream of a famous scientist with a head injury. Their mission is to travel in a miniature submarine to his brain and repair the injury with laser beams. A climactic scene calls for the doctors to leave their sub and "swim" through the scientist's brain. As you can see in the photograph, if ever a set was designed to hide telltale support wires, this was it!

This brain set was gigantic — over five million times the size of the average human brain. Rather than flood this set with water and film the actors actually swimming through the "body fluid," the scene was filmed dry. The mechanical-effects crew hooked the actors up to wires and moved them from above while the actors made swimming motions in the air. The cameras filmed this scene with high-speed filming — shooting at three times the normal speed — and on screen, the rescuers appear to be swimming through a thick liquid.

Strands of piano wire are well hidden in this "swimming" scene from Fantastic Voyage. *(© 1966, Twentieth Century-Fox)*

Both pod and astronaut are dangled from the starry ceiling by lengths of wire in Kubrick's famed space opera, 2001: A Space Odyssey. *Because the camera is shooting directly up, the wires are hidden from view by the pod and the astronaut's own body. (Copyright © 1968, MGM; Museum of Modern Art/ Film Stills Archive)*

Wires were kept from the camera's eye in another clever way in *2001: A Space Odyssey* (1968). The astronaut and the space pod shown in the photograph were suspended from high ceiling beams by piano wire. What made this shot tricky was that both the astronaut and the pod were attached to the wires on their *sides*. The camera was then placed below and off to one side, so that their unattached sides could be filmed. With this setup, the pod and the astronaut's own body were between the camera and the wires and so they hid them perfectly.

Actors who are wired up for flying, floating, or swimming scenes wear special "flying harnesses" made of heavy canvas lined with sheep's wool so that they won't develop any sore spots. These harnesses are worn under costumes, of course, and if the actors are under the hot studio lights, they can quickly lose their cool. Many times a tired, overheated actor will have to hang for hours and hours up in the air while a scene is shot several times. It's safe to bet that even for Superman, who "flew" with Lois Lane in the Metropolis scenes suspended from a crane that was 250 feet high, working on wires wasn't such a snap.

Piano wire has been used to make bats fly in low-budget vampire films and to dangle actual cars over cliffs in suspenseful thrillers. Piano wire was reponsible for holding up the Cowardly Lion's tail in *The Wizard of Oz* and for making it twitch. It also supported the chief extraterrestrial visitor in *Close Encounters of the Third Kind;* it was manipulated by eight puppeteers in the rafters over the set. In fact, piano wire is used so much in movie making that a story is told about a Hollywood accountant who received several bills for piano wire during the production of a certain film. He paid the bills, but after he saw the movie, he went to the director to complain because, he said, he hadn't *seen* any piano wire in the film at all!

ROBOT CONTROL

The producers of *Star Wars* spent an astronomical one hundred thousand dollars just developing and making the robot R2D2. Several different R2D2 models were actually used in the movie. A miniature was photographed in long shots while a "drone," or a prop robot without any moving parts, was filmed in scenes where no movement was required. The most famous robot was inhabited by a 3'8" actor named Kenny Baker. But because the robot frame itself weighed more than a hundred pounds, it was hard for Baker to scoot about quickly in it and so a fourth type of robot was built to be operated by *remote control.*

Remote control is a method of moving things from a distance by means of radio waves. You may have seen small model planes that are flown by on-the-ground operators with remote-control mechanisms. The advantage of remote control over piano wire is obvious — radio waves won't ever show up on the screen. But as a method of moving action props, it's strictly a lightweight operation: remote control simply won't work for heavy loads. It worked well for the little R2D2, however, which was constructed to weigh as little as possible and move smoothly and easily on wheels.

Remote control was also used to solve a "high fashion" dilemma in *Superman.* In flying scenes when Superman was dangled from a crane or supported in front of a blue screen, his cape hung down by his sides unconvincingly. The first answer to this problem was to aim huge fans at Superman, but this caused the cape to cling to his body and didn't give the desired billowing effect. Finally a device consisting of batteries and two fishing-rod-like extensions was invented for actor Chris Reeves to wear underneath the collar of his Superman cape. No matter where he had to "fly," effects men could control the swirl in his cape from the ground below by using a remote-control system to raise and lower the "fishing rods."

HEAVY-DUTY AIR

Pulleys, wires, remote control — all of these prop-moving methods are used for the small-size jobs. When it comes to the big jobs, *air* is often used — air that is put under pressure. Air pressure is what operates *pneumatic machines.* The hand pump you use to put air into a bike tire is a pneumatic machine. It takes in air, squeezes it into a contained space — your tire — and, as you pump, it keeps squeezing in air until the tire is inflated. The air in the tire is under a lot of pressure — that's what keeps the tire extended. If you get a hole in your tire, you may have a "blow out," which is a kind of explosion and proof of the power of compressed air. It is just this air power that mechanical-effects experts often use to mobilize their monsters.

Jaws is a movie about a shark with a hearty appetite. The shark invades the offshore waters of a resort town at the height of the tourist season and makes a practice of dining on swimmers. To be sure, playing the starring role in *Jaws* was something that an aspiring Great White shark could really sink its teeth into. However, the film's human actors could hardly be expected to do swimming scenes with a live twenty-five-foot shark, and so a mechanical shark star — fondly called Bruce after the director's lawyer — was born.

This fiendish creation of effects expert Bob Mattey was really a triple threat: three sharks were built, each with a different role to play. Bruce I was actually only fifteen feet long — mostly mouth and head. Since he was used only for straight-on swimming scenes, no one noticed his shortened tail section. When a shark with a handsome left profile was needed, Bruce II was called into action. This twenty-five-foot shark had a complete head and left side. His right side, however, which never turned toward the camera, was open, ex-

The mechanical shark star of Jaws *just can't seem to get enough of the tourist trade. (Copyright © Universal City Studios, Inc. All rights reserved.)*

Bruce II reveals the inside story of the shark from Jaws. *(Photograph from* The Making of the Movie "Jaws" *by Edith Blake, copyright © 1975 by Edith Blake. Published by Ballantine Books, Inc. Reprinted by permission.)*

posing his "guts"—hundreds of feet of steel tubing and pneumatic hose. Bruce III was the mirror image of Bruce II, his head and right side being complete, while his left side was open.

Bruce I was a "floater," designed to be pulled through the water by a speeding boat out of the camera's range. Bruces II and III were hooked up on their open sides to a long, crane-like arm. This arm was connected to an underwater cart which moved along a track laid on the ocean's floor. This arm propelled the sharks across the surface of the water something like an undersea railroad. But to make the sharks move their fins, thrash their tails, open their mouths, roll their eyes, and chomp on their victims, pneumatic equipment was needed. Some twenty cables and hoses ran from Bruce II's open side, for example, to a boat anchored just out of the camera's view. From this boat, four people pushed and pulled levers that made Bruce go into his shark act. The pneumatic hoses worked something like the small party favors that are all curled up until you blow into them and then they stick straight out. In a similar way, Bruce's operators pulled levers that sent strong gusts of compressed air rushing through the pneumatic hoses. The air pressure moved various valves in Bruce's head, face, and fins to make him look like the real thing.

All told, it took Mattey and his team six months to build the terrible trio and they took a whopping two-hundred-thousand-dollar bite out of the budget. Yet, throughout the shooting of *Jaws*, Bruce acted like a temperamental star, requiring much attention. The first time the ton-and-a-half mechanical shark went before the cameras, it sank like a rock. On the second try, its eyes crossed and its mouth jammed open. When the jaws finally did snap shut, the shark, it was noticed, had a double chin. Another time Bruce went out of control and attacked his own operating platform, severely smashing his snout. Even the shark's skin — made of molded plastic covered with polyurethane and nylon and then sandblasted to give it the rough texture of true sharkskin — proved to be a problem. The harsh salt water decomposed it and barnacles grew in several spots, ruining Bruce's complexion so that his skin had to be totally replaced every week during shooting. Bruce also required not one but two sets of false teeth: a hard plastic set for gnawing on boats and a soft rubber set for "chewing up" stunt people.

Of course, the *Jaws* film crew wanted Bruce to look as convincing as possible up on the big screen. One of the secrets of filming a mechanical model so that it looks real is quick cutting from the mechanical monster to an *actual* monster — provided that one is available. A flesh-and-blood shark *was* used in many scenes in *Jaws*. The idea was that the beginning of the movie would show the real shark in several scenes that did not require any interaction between the shark and the human actors. These first shots let the audience know that there was indeed a real shark lurking just offshore. Once the shark was established as real, when someone had to be eaten up, a quick switch was made, and Bruce appeared on the screen to do the chewing.

The real shark that Universal found to play the part was only twelve feet long — thirteen feet shorter than it was supposed to be. Its "puny" size didn't matter in shots where the shark was seen swimming alone — it looked plenty big and plenty fierce. But its size did pose a problem in the scene where the shark expert, played by Richard Dreyfuss, descended in a diving cage to battle the shark. When they were seen together in the same shot, it was clear that the shark was only twice as big as Dreyfuss rather than four times his size. In order to make the shark appear much bigger, a midget stunt man was hired to double for Dreyfuss. He wore scaled-down scuba gear and was lowered in a scaled-down diving cage for his scenes with the shark. He was so small that, by comparison, he made the shark look twice as big.

Another trick used in photographing action props is cutting very quickly away from a mechanical model to other action-packed scenes in the movie. Unfortunately, the makers of *Jaws* didn't follow this rule. Instead, they let their cameras focus too long and lovingly on Bruce. In the movie's climactic scene, where the shark devours an experienced shark hunter, played by Robert Shaw — a scene which, by the way, took two full days to shoot — Bruce is on screen for so long that he begins to look more like an amusement park version of a shark than a true terror of the deep.

After the harsh criticism of the mechanical shark in the otherwise good reviews of *Jaws*, the producers decided to spruce Bruce up for *Jaws II* (1978). Mattey's refurbishing took two whole years and cost over two million dollars. Bruce could do a few more stunts than before, such as turning in a full circle, but along the way he and his rig gained a little weight — some thirteen tons in all — which made him sluggish. And, if you saw *Jaws II*, you know that the shark looked just about the same way it did in *Jaws* — like a mechanical monster.

But the end of this fish story is that it didn't seem to matter *what* the shark looked like — both *Jaws* movies were super-blockbusters. Just the *idea* of a renegade shark feasting on innocent swimmers was scary enough to keep many people out of the water — and in line for the movies — for a long, long time.

Kong, as you know, was a miniature. At least the *whole* Kong was. But parts of the great ape were anything *but* miniature and, rather than being animated frame by frame, these full-scale parts of King Kong were activated by pneumatic power.

By building a giant bust, arm and hand section, and foot of Kong,

Fay Wray is actually in the full-scale hand, but the camera is positioned so that we look over the shoulder of the miniature King Kong. In this way, the miniature Kong "stood in" for the thirty-foot ape in the 1933 production of King Kong. *(The Collection of Orville Goldner)*

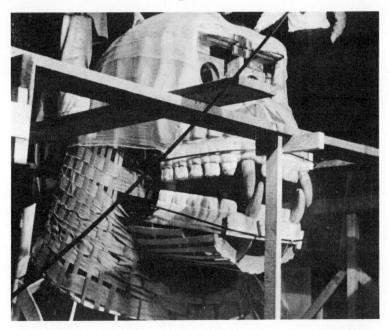

The full-scale head of Kong in construction for King Kong, *1933. (The Collection of Orville Goldner)*

the film makers didn't have to rely on miniature rear-projection or matte shots to show the ape interacting with people. They filmed many close-up shots of Fay Wray, for example, struggling and screaming in the giant-size paw that was built. Then, in the editing room, these scenes were intercut with scenes of the miniature Kong holding a tiny Fay Wray doll. In this way, the film makers created the illusion that the eighteen-inch miniature model and the full-scale hand belonged to the same giant ape. Fay Wray described her "close encounters" with the huge paw this way:

> The hand and arm in which my close-up scenes were made was about eight feet in length. Inside the furry arm there was a steel bar and the whole contraption (with me in the hand) could be raised and low-ered like a crane. The fingers would be pressed around my waist while I was in a standing position. I would then be raised about ten feet in the air, to be in line with an elevated camera. As I kicked and squirmed and

struggled in the ape's hand, his fingers would gradually loosen and
begin to open. My fear was real as I grabbed on to his wrist, his thumb,
whatever I could to keep from slipping out of that paw!

Happily, the situation never got "out of hand" and Fay Wray was
always lowered to the ground before she could fall.

The full-scale foot of Kong was merely a prop, but the head section, like the arm and hand, had many moving parts. This immense
head, as it is described in *The Making of King Kong*, was made of
wood, metal, and cloth and was covered on the outside by bearskin.
Kong's balsa-wood-and-plaster eyes were a foot wide each. Kong's
nose was two feet across, and his teeth were up to ten inches long.
His mouth was wide enough to gobble down several stunt men in a
single bite. The whole prop was mounted on a heavy cart with
wheels so that it could be moved about. Three operators actually
stayed inside Kong's head and, with pneumatic levers, were able to
move the mouth, lips, nose, eyes, eyelids, and eyebrows to give
incredibly real expressions.

WATER-PRESSURE WONDERS

Hydraulic pressure is another way that mechanical creations can be
made to move. Instead of working on air pressure, hydraulic machines work on water or liquid pressure. When you squeeze the
trigger of a water pistol, you are using hydraulic pressure to squirt
someone. The idea of hydraulics is, very basically, that a little bit of
pressure connected to a hydraulic system can lift a great deal of
weight. If your dentist or your haircutter pumps a hydraulic foot
lever on a chair several times, he or she can lift you up higher with
very little effort.

Colin Chilvers, who created the marvelous physical effects for
Superman, had this to say about hydraulics: "Hydraulics is really a liquid which, when used with the right equipment, is such a powerful
force that there's practically nothing you can't move with it. It just
fascinates me that simply by pressing a little lever or button, you can
lift fifty tons. It creates a power complex. . ."

It was hydraulic power that was responsible for the incredible
Krypton-quake that destroyed Superman's home planet. The hy-
draulic equipment was designed to fit underneath the floor of the
Krypton set. On a given signal, operators off camera began pressing

Hydraulic pressure helps Superbaby show off for his Earthly parents in Superman. *(TM and © 1979 DC Comics Inc.)*

buttons that activated machinery which actually lifted the entire set to make it shake and rock itself to pieces. (This same hydraulic setup was also used to shake things up in certain scenes in *Earthquake*.)

Hydraulics, too, can operate movie monsters. A mechanical sea creature created by Bob Mattey that got better reviews than Bruce from *Jaws* was the giant squid on Disney's *20,000 Leagues Under the Sea* (1954). This movie centers on the adventures of a crazed Captain Nemo and the unwilling "guests" aboard his fantastic submarine, the *Nautilus*. A high point in the film occurs when a gigantic squid attacks and the crew members must come out of the sub to engage the squid in gueling hand-to-tentacle combat.

Sixteen men operated the squid's sucker-lined hydraulic tentacles. They became so skilled at flailing these dangerous appendages about that, according to some sources, they could capture a *Nautilus* sailor by whipping a tentacle around him, much like a cowpoke ropes a steer. But to ensure 100 per cent accuracy, the real takes *began* with

Operators pull hydraulic levers to make Disney's giant squid menace seamen in 20,000 Leagues Under the Sea. *(© 1954, Disney Studios)*

the tentacles already wrapped around the victims. Then, as the cameras rolled, the operators *unwrapped* the tentacles from the actors. The film was printed in *reverse* and the finished scene shows the squid reaching out for its enemies and wrapping them up with chilling realism.

The fight between the *Nautilus* crew and the squid wasn't filmed at sea, as the scenes with the *Jaws* shark were. Instead, it was filmed in the Disney studio's enormous tank. Yet both the stormy "ocean" and the angry squid looked terrifyingly real and helped to win Mattey a well-deserved Oscar for Special Effects.

Not only is hydraulic machinery capable of moving great weights, but it is also used when great precision and finely detailed movements are needed. It supplied the necessary agility to the squid's tentacles and it was also used to give expression to Kong's face in the 1976 remake of *King Kong*. In this version of the film, a man in a monkey suit *was* used to play Kong. Normally, this wouldn't be considered a mechanical effect, but in this case, the face of the monkey

The squid's hydraulically controlled tentacle easily picks up a Nautilus *crew member in a fight to the finish. (© 1954, Disney Studios)*

A huge mechanical- action prop kept actress Jessica Lange firmly in hand in the 1976 remake of King Kong. *(© 1976, Paramount Pictures)*

suit was a mask with an interchangeable set of seven different hydraulically controlled faces. The different expressions were controlled by cables which ran out of the back of the neck of the mask and were attached to a control panel just off camera. There, operators pulled levers which changed the small features on this little ape's face to make him look angry, gleeful, or puzzled.

A huge, full-scale arm and hand were also constructed for the 1976 remake of King Kong. The base of the enormous arm was a steel "skeleton" covered with foam rubber. A fur "coat" made of Argentine horsetails was fastened around the huge arm and hand by one of the world's largest zippers. The hand had a central cable running through it with sixteen hydraulic jacks—similar in principle to the power jacks used to raise cars that have flat tires. Four men at a control panel operated the jacks. Each jack moved a different part of Kong's hand. To get ready for a shot, the operators would flex the huge hand in the air, making it look like the hand of some gigantic hairy pianist warming up for a piece. Each of Kong's big knuckles had a safety bolt inside it so that if one of the hydraulic operators accidentally pressed a lever too far in the wrong direction, the hand still wouldn't squeeze actress Jessica Lange too hard.

The most important factor in operating a mechanical prop like Kong's hand or the giant squid is timing. When the director gives a direction, all of the people operating controls must respond to it at exactly the same time or the whole effect will be thrown off.

IMAGINATION POWER

Mechanical-effects aces have even more up their sleeves than the tricks mentioned here. In addition to building and operating props that are worked by pulleys, remote controls, wires, pneumatics, and hydraulics, they must also know how to rig up dump tanks that unleash thousands of gallons of water on a scene, blow up buildings, and do whatever else a job calls for—which, in the field of mechanical special effects, can be just about anything at all.

6

Crash! Bam! Boom!
Live-Action Effects

One of the most memorable scenes in the 1974 disaster epic *Earthquake* takes place when the big quake hits and buildings start to collapse, raining rubble and debris on the people in the streets. What appeared on screen was mass mayhem, with terrified passersby scuttling for safety from huge falling chunks of concrete, pieces of steel, and heavy signs. Yet in reality there was no danger; the "chaos" was as carefully choreographed as any ballet.

First, the action was carefully plotted out on paper to show where everyone had to be at each moment. Then the scene was rehearsed very slowly so that each actor knew exactly what path to follow and exactly how much time he had to reach his destination. Fifty-five special-effects men were on hand, each one responsible for just a small bit of action and for just one actor's safety. Thus, an effects man had to know that when a certain actor reached point X, he had to hit the switch that would make a column break or send a pane of glass hurtling out a window.

This kind of split-second timing is crucial in complicated live-action scenes where real risk is involved and one wrong move can cause an honest-to-goodness catastrophe. What is required is precision teamwork between seasoned special-effects experts and experienced professional stunt people.

Stunt men and women, looking appropriately terrified, dodge falling debris in a carefully choreographed scene from Earthquake. *(Copyright © Universal City Studios, Inc. All rights reserved.)*

The last decade's flood of disaster flicks has meant steady work for Hollywood's corps of professional daredevils, who have been drowned by giant waves in *The Poseidon Adventure*, squashed to death in *Earthquake*, and burnt to a crisp in *The Towering Inferno*.

GAGS

Stunts, or "gags" as they are called in the trade, are no laughing matter. In *The Towering Inferno* many people actually were set on fire and really did plunge off the skyscraper set. These feats are relatively safe, however, because they are performed by professionals who have developed certain specialties over the years. Some stunters have built their careers by doing high falls, for example; others by crashing cars or performing horse tricks and still others by turning themselves into human torches (this stunt, one of the most dangerous of all, is known as a "full burn").

The trick in all of these stunts is to minimize the danger in real life and maximize it on the screen. This is where the talents of special-effects experts come into play. First of all, they make all sorts of special props which heighten the sense of danger and realism in live-action scenes for moviegoers. Secondly, they have perfected safety devices, hidden from the camera's eye, for the protection of stunt people. And lastly, they know how (and are specifically licensed) to handle dangerous materials such as explosives, which are often used in live-action scenes.

BREAKING UP IS EASY TO DO

At least half of all motion-picture props are made to be broken. These "self-destruct" items, known as breakaways, include such props as glass windows, bottles, dishes, chairs, and tables.

In the early days of motion pictures, sugar was the main ingredient in "candy" glass. It was used whenever a character had to crash through a window. Candy glass did not break into dangerously sharp points and, after a stunt was over, the actor could nibble on the delicious "shards." Candy glass was made by dissolving lots of sugar into a little boiling water; then the liquid solution was poured into a flat "pane." Of course, candy glass was much thicker than real glass and not nearly as clear, so when a scene called for a crash through a window, the real window would be shown in all shots except the final one when the stunter made the actual leap through the "glass."

Another drawback to candy glass was that it tended to melt under hot studio lights. Today fake glass is made from special thin, clear plastics which are not only more durable, but much more realistic.

Breakaway bottles, a must in any Western with a good, old-fashioned barroom brawl, can be made by pouring paraffin wax into a mold in the shape of a bottle. The liquid wax is swished around until it has coated the entire inside of the mold. The rest is poured out, producing a hollow cast. When the wax has cooled and hardened, the mold is opened and — voilá — a translucent fragile bottle

A stuntman hurtles through a window of harmless "candy glass" in The Towering Inferno. *(Copyright © 1974, Twentieth Century-Fox)*

that will break into harmless pieces the second it is bopped over someone's head.

Paraffin mixed with fine chalk powder or even with dry plaster can be molded into realistic dishware and china. Plates or vases can also be made from a mixture of plaster and ground-up Styrofoam which is modeled by hand and then carved to create the finished product. Dishes, especially plates, can also be created by baking raw dough—just as you would a real pie!

As for breakaway furniture, it is made from soft balsa wood and held together either by glue or toothpick "dowels." (Nails and screws might really hurt an intended victim.)

The fall of a wall, the cave-in of a roof, or the collapse of an entire building also "fall" within the province of special-effects props. For safety, lightweight materials are used — either cardboard, papier mâche, or plastics such as Styrofoam. In *Earthquake* the falling chunks of "concrete" from the violently shaking skyscraper were made of Styrofoam but they were far from harmless. That's because they were heavily weighted inside with steel so they would crash to the ground realistically. If any stunter had been hit, serious injuries could have resulted. That's why proper safety precautions are so important in filming scenes of dangerous live action. But it wasn't always that way.

SAFETY FIRST

In the infant days of film making, few safety measures were taken in setting up dangerous stunts that were performed by amateurs at their own risk — usually extras who were in need of a fast buck. For the incredible harum-scarum car chases in his Keystone Kops comedies, director Mack Sennett would simply throw soapy water on the roads to make the skids more lively. And for D. W. Griffith's silent extravaganza, *Intolerance* (1916), the extras, who got a measly $5.00 to plummet off the high walls of Babylon, had only a bale of hay or the like to break their fall.

Safety standards on movie sets today are so high, and serious mishaps so rare, that premiums on accident insurance for stunt people are surprisingly low. This is partially due to the precautions taken by special-effects men to protect stunters.

Nowadays, for example, when a stunt person takes a high fall, huge 15' × 20' air bags are spread out to cushion the fall. This safety device, or "rig" as it is called, works so well in movie stunts that it is starting to be used in real fire-rescue work.

Crashing cars is also a risky business. The stunt driver has to figure out mathematically exactly how fast the car must go in order to hit another car at just the right moment and at just the right place (crashes are planned so that one car hits another from the side, since head-on collisions are the most dangerous). The risk of danger is also reduced by the protective gear and devices used in these stunts. Drivers wear seat belts, knee and elbow pads, and even helmets if

Professional stunt woman Betty Danko doubles for Margaret Hamilton in the Wicked Witch's flying scenes from The Wizard of Oz. *(MGM, 1939; Museum of Modern Art/Film Stills Archive)*

they can go undetected by the camera. The insides of the cars are padded, too; any sharp objects are removed; and sometimes the windshield is taken out. If the car is going downhill the battery is removed and if the car has to roll over, the inside of the roof is reinforced with steel plates called a "roll bar," so that the roof can't cave in and crush the driver inside. Lastly, to cut down the chance of fire, just enough gas is put in to get through the stunt.

Of course, sometimes stunt people are purposely set on fire. A "full burn" not only takes the raw guts of stunt people to let themselves be set ablaze, but also the careful planning of special-effects crews to avert disaster.

In *The Towering Inferno* a group of hapless victims are shown caught in an elevator, their clothes and hair on fire. The stunters who played the human matchsticks were outfitted in airtight fireproof underwear and clothes, face masks and fireproof wigs, and they each had hidden miniaturized breathing equipment—air tanks like those scuba divers have, but on a smaller scale—with three minutes supply of air. Right before the scene was shot, their clothes were painted with a mixture of gasoline and alcohol and then set afire. The cameras rolled, showing the victims up close, and then, the moment the

A blaze that seems out of control on screen is actually carefully controlled by special-effects coordinators in Grand Prix. *(MGM, 1966; Museum of Modern Art/Film Stills Archive)*

Full-scale flames leap high over the heads of actors Clark Gable and Vivien Leigh in the famous burning-of-Atlanta scene from Gone With the Wind. *(Copyright © MGM; Museum of Modern ART/Film Stills Archive)*

scene was over, the stunters were hosed down with CO_2. And as when all such fire scenes were filmed, firemen also stood by just in case anything went wrong.

Special-effects crews are also in charge of burning up buildings. In *The Towering Inferno*, a seventy-foot-high miniature of the skyscraper was set ablaze. This was seen in long shots with quick cuts to the live-action scenes where there were full-scale sections of sets on fire.

The standard method for making fire is to pipe butane, propane, or liquid petroleum gas from tanks which are outside the camera's range to jets hidden in back of the set. A keyboard controls the jets so that special-effects men can, for example, turn up the flames pouring out of the different windows of a building and get exactly the kind of inferno they want.

Usually the full-scale sets or miniatures are painted with fire-re-retardant paint. This way they won't be consumed entirely if repeated takes are necessary or if the sets are needed for several scenes. The idea is to give the appearance of a conflagration while actually burning only very small areas of the sets.

The burning of Atlanta in *Gone With the Wind* (1939) was handled very differently, however. The full-size sets of building fronts were set on fire by piping in a thousand gallons of fuel per minute. The fire leaped hundreds of feet into the air and in six minutes the "city" was actually burned to the ground. The on-screen effect is dazzling, but playing with fire this way was risky indeed. The director had to be confident that everything would go perfectly on the very first take. If it hadn't, the whole scene would have literally gone up in smoke!

it's dynamite!

The use of explosives also falls under the category of fire effects and is more carefully regulated than any other kind of special effects. To become a qualified explosives handler, a person must first have two and a half years of experience as a prop handler (a prop handler is often nicknamed "green man" since the work involves moving around a lot of shrubbery). This basic apprenticeship is followed by 1,500 hours performing ordinary special effects such as creating fake frost or a rainstorm, then an explosives course, approved by the State of California, and a security clearance by the FBI to make sure that the explosives will not fall into the wrong hands. After all of this, the applicant becomes a Class Three powderman and is licensed to handle explosives on movie sets.

The most obvious use of explosives is for war epics where cannons are firing and bombs are bursting. But explosives also come in handy for triggering volcanic eruptions, exploding cars on impact, and riddling an actor with "bullet holes."

A "bullet hit" is a small protective metal plate with a groove in the middle. Into the groove goes a small explosive cap and beside that a sac of fake blood. The metal plate is mounted on a leather patch and either strapped to the actor's body or sewn onto his underclothing. A wire runs from the cap underneath the actor's clothes and out of the camera's range, where it is set off electrically by a special-effects man. On cue he can fire off the explosive, thereby breaking the blood bag, burning a hole in the actor's clothes and causing a realistic "wound."

Effects experts know exactly where to place these charges so that they won't harm the wired-up actor. This method is infinitely safer than the early twenties technique of hiring crack riflemen who shot live ammo, sometimes aiming only inches away from the understandably jittery actors.

To fake exploding mines, artillery shells, and other land explosions that are part and parcel of every war flick, special-effects experts make "bombs" out of cone-shaped steel pots that are filled with an explosive such as black powder and covered with a layer of cork or peat moss to simulate flying dirt, rocks, and other debris.

The site for each explosion has to be carefully picked out by the special-effects man. The "bombs" are then planted in dug-out holes and topped with fuller's earth (a claylike substance) that matches the color of the ground. In this way, the "bombs" are hidden from the camera's view. The holes also guarantee that the force of the explosion will go upward, giving both a safe and spectacular stunt.

Sometimes a small trampoline is placed behind a small hill so that it can't be seen by the camera. At the moment when a bomb goes off, a stunt man can jump on the trampoline and hurtle up into the air. What the shocked audience sees is a soldier apparently blown sky-high by an explosion.

Of course, none of this is left to guesswork. The special-effects man works very closely with the director, cameraman, stunt coordinator who's in charge of planning "gags," and naturally the stunters themselves so that audiences can be treated to the kind of live-action scenes that have provided some of the most bone-chilling, heart-stopping moments in movie history.

7

Fooling Mother Nature: Weather Effects

It may not be nice to fool Mother Nature, but Hollywood effects technicians have been doing it for a long time: whether a movie script calls for blinding blizzards or a light flurry of snowfall, desert sandstorms or tropical monsoon rains, a 100-m.p.h. tornado or just a gentle summer breeze, special-effects experts have proved that they can weather anything, producing extraordinarily real atmospheric conditions on screen.

In fact, whenever specific climate conditions are called for in a movie, the great outdoors is almost always recreated inside a sound-studio stage. It's easy to see why a production unit would rather remain in Hollywood and whip up a fake snowstorm than spend lots of time and money to take cast, crew and cameras on location to Siberia. But why do special-effects men bother to create made-to-order weather for such everyday commodities as clouds or rain? Quite simply, it's because real weather is far too unpredictable and uncontrollable. Let's say a director is filming a horror movie—*The House on Haunted Hill*. A perfect hill has been found with a nice spooky house right smack on top of it. All that's needed now for the climactic scene is an average, run-of-the-mill thunderstorm. The forecasts have predicted one, so the director sets up his cameras, gets the cast ready and waits. . . and waits. . . and waits. Maybe fortune smiles and the storm hits. The cameras roll and film some frightening flashes of lightning—only the storm ends way before the scene does and the director is left with depressingly unscary blue skies.

When special-effects teams create the environment nothing is left to chance. The weather can be forecast with complete accuracy. If periodic rains are called for with heavy clouds and light gusting winds, that's just what will appear on screen and these "conditions" can last for as long as a scene requires.

IN A FOG

Oddly enough, another reason weather is created is that man-made atmospheric effects sometimes photograph even more realistically than the genuine article. Famous London fog, for example, isn't very photogenic at all. On screen it looks more like dense smoke, thick and almost impossible to see through. The film crew working on a little-known movie called *The Amateur Gentleman* (1936) found this out after trying to shoot a scene of a dramatic prison break under cover of London fog. In the end the scene had to be reshot in a studio using smoke from a chemically treated wood powder which, when lit, gave off a very convincing "fog." And so the problem of fog that looked like smoke was solved by substituting a smoke that looked like fog!

Creating fog—anything from a fine mist to one of pea-soup thickness—is the most common atmospheric effect that special-effects experts create. After all, it's a "must" for almost any horror movie.

Creating fog can be done in a number of ways. Today the easiest but crudest technique is to use a fog filter. This is a special piece of "foggy" ground glass which, when placed over a camera lens, fuzzes up the photographed image. The problem is that "fog" from filters has no depth or natural drift, so it's only used for quick close-up shots.

For low-hanging ground fog, a much more lifelike effect is achieved by placing dry ice in a trough of hot water. The resulting "fog cloud" hugs the ground and, with gentle fanning, can flow in any direction. Unfortunately, dry-ice fog doesn't last long and, more importantly, it can be dangerous. The carbon dioxide released in dry-ice fog can be harmful to animals on the set or to anyone who is lying on the ground. Therefore, dry-ice fog is used only under very controlled circumstances, when the air can be cleared quickly of the harmful carbon dioxide.

The most advanced — and safest — way to have a good fog roll in is to use fog machines available from motion picture or theatrical supply houses. The standard type can give off anything from light haze to impenetrable ocean fog. (Fog machines also create the billowing smoke for burning buildings or forest fires.)

After being filled with a tank of Fog Juice — a special type of mineral oil — the machine is plugged in to activate a heating element. The oil mixture is warmed and vaporized until it becomes tiny particles which, when released into the air through a nozzle, condense into a white vapor. All the fog-machine operator has to do is plug in the machine, push a plunger and — whoosh — out comes the fog.

A Mole-Richardson Fog Maker fills a set with a thick fog. Inside the machine is an oil-based liquid called Fog Juice which vaporizes when heated to produce fantastic fog. (Photo courtesy Warren K. Parker, President, Mole-Richardson Co., Hollywood, California, U.S.A.)

Fog-machine fog is quite harmless unless people breathe in quite a lot of it. And just as quickly as the fog comes, it can be made to "lift" and disappear by spraying special "Fog Chaser" liquid from the same fog machine.

When miniature sets are being used, small, exceptionally realistic banks of clouds can be formed in much the same way that machine-made fog is created. A substance called Britt-Smoke is sprayed from a double-nozzle spray gun and out pour perfect, puffy cloud heads. Britt Smoke cannot be used around actors, however, because it's highly acidic and thus potentially dangerous.

Clouds can also be formed optically with glass shots and matte paintings. Or, if there's a rush job, special-effects men can resort to quickie methods. For *The Trollenberg Terror* a grade Z sci-fi flick of the 1950s, a respected British effects man who had little time and even less money had to create a cloud on top of a mountain. His short-cut technique was simply to take a wad of absorbent cotton and stick it to a photograph of a mountain. The effect, to be charitable, was less than convincing, but the photo appears several times in the movie. Whenever an actor stares out a window, the camera cuts to the mountain with the cotton stuck in a new position.

RAINMAKING

Of course, studio-made clouds never release any rain, so that, too, must be manufactured by special effects artists. In *The Rains Came* (1939), which takes place in India, ten thousands gallons of water poured down each minute the movie's climactic deluge was being filmed. That adds up to an average rainfall of forty inches a day!

While real rain can cause exasperating delays to film units on location, fake rain can be tricky to deal with, too. When filming is being done indoors in sound stages, an overhead sprinkler system can rain down on the set with various size sprinkler heads providing anything from a light drizzle to a torrential downpour. Special-effects men have to be extremely careful about containing this "rain." Usually a sheet of plastic spread on the floor acts as a catch basin to keep the water away from electrical wiring and camera equipment until it is drained away.

For shooting outdoors, fire hoses, which are out of the camera's range, are squirted high up in the sky with the "precipitation" falling back to earth. The key factor here is to make it look like it's raining throughout the scene, not just in the foreground. This requires many hoses, which are moved back and forth slightly so that the downpour doesn't look unnaturally even.

Wind machines are also used to blow "rain" about. Basically just big electric fans mounted on stands, wind machines are not only indispensable for routine breezes and gusts, they're also used in many kinds of storm sequences.

Special winds—tornadoes, typhoons, and the like—require more special effects. One of the most inventive feats was the making of the tornado in *The Wizard of Oz*. Arnold Gillespie, in charge of special effects for the movie, tried many ways of photographing the great whirlwind that takes Dorothy to the land of Oz, but every one looked phony until he hit upon the ingenious idea of blowing air from a fan through a woman's stocking. The resulting miniature "twister" was so realistic that for years MGM used this footage in other movies with tornadoes in them.

The tropical storm that was the climax of the original version of *The Hurricane* (1937) is a good example of how wind and rain machines and a slew of other special-effects devices were put to work to create twenty minutes of sound and fury on screen. *The Hurricane* was a lot like the popular disaster movies of the 1970s (this is probably why producer Dino De Laurentiis decided to do a remake called *Hurricane* in 1979). A star-studded cast was wasted on a silly story about corrupt white men on an unspoiled South Sea island while the real star of the show was a no-holds-barred hurricane which practically wipes the tiny island of Manakua right off the map.

The storm finale, which still draws gasps from audiences, took nearly four months to film and was made entirely on a studio back lot. A life-size native village with wharves, thatched huts, palm trees, a beachfront, and a church was built facing onto a calm "lagoon" (the Goldwyn studio tank). For the storm, roller waves—pistons that move up and down—churned the placid waters of the studio tank into big breakers. Hefty three-inch-wide-fire hoses drenched the "island" and all its inhabitants; and airplane motors mounted on

Dorothy, and Toto, too, are blown by giant wind fans as they attempt to escape from Gillespie's stocking cyclone in The Wizard of Oz. *(MGM, 1939; Museum of Modern Art/Film Stills Archive)*

stands whipped up a wind of hurricane force. The crowning blow, however, was a giant wave produced by unleashing two thousand gallons of water into the lagoon from dump tanks. Dump tanks are special tanks with chutes, built on the sides of studio tanks. They can release very large amounts of water very suddenly. The force of all of this cascading water is tremendous—and dangerous—but there were no real casualties of the hurricane, which crumpled houses, bent palm trees over double, and ripped off the church steeple. The final tab for the hurricane sequence was $400,000—$150,000 to build the island village and $250,000 to destroy it!

The special-effects crew on a pirate movie called *High Wind in Jamaica* (1966) was so busy setting up for a simulated storm that had to level a house that they missed the real storm that unexpectedly hit the Caribbean island. The head of the special-effects crew was understandably furious at this missed opportunity.

The members of a California film unit on a movie called *The Sky Pilot* (1921) were really on their toes. When a freak early-fall snowstorm hit the outdoor set of a town, the crew decided to film the movie's winter scenes ahead of schedule. Their plan was then to let the snow melt and finish the remaining summer scenes . . . only the cold weather didn't let up. Finally the crew shoveled off all of the snow so that they could film the rest of the "warm weather" snowless scenes. Then they waited patiently for more snow to fall, because the climactic finale of the movie involved the total destruction of the snow-covered town by fire. But now, of course, it refused to snow! Eventually the frustrated crew had to resort to artificial snow — in this case, tons of salt — to recreate their winter wonderland!

SNOW BUSINESS

Historically, special-effects men have used almost anything white, light, and flaky for fake snow, including chips of balsa wood, powdered detergent, and even chopped feathers until it was discovered that they could cause serious lung damage when inhaled.

In one movie fake snow even caused real colds! The reason for the mysterious rash of respiratory infections was finally traced to the dust in the mixture of gypsum and cornflakes used for the snow. The cure was for all of the cast and crew to don surgical masks at all times except during the actual filming.

Bleached cornflakes were a very popular substitute for real snowflakes even though they often bounced instead of gently falling to the ground and they required periodic fumigation to get rid of hibernating insects. With the arrival of "the talkies," however, came the most serious drawback to using cereal snow — it crunched!

For the past twenty years or so special-effects departments have often relied on plastic snowflakes made by shredding polyethylene bags like the ones used by dry cleaners. The shredded plastic is pounded in a hammer mill, which causes a chemical reaction that changes its color from clear to pure white. Plastic snow can be blown

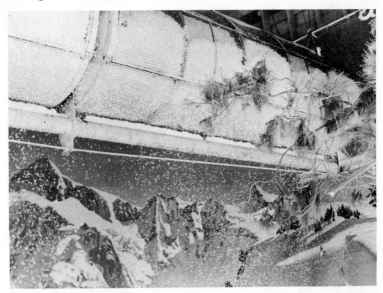

A large drum filled with polyethylene snow rotates to create a blizzard.
(Photo copyright © 1978 Rita Miami)

about by wind machines or poured into snow machines—long, deep tanks with narrow slotted openings at the bottom—that are suspended over the set to release the falling snow.

Of course, this plastic snow doesn't melt and it takes a lot of shoveling to clean up after a storm. So for some indoor blizzards, special-effects men use water mixed with a foaming agent (it's very much like fire extinguisher foam) which, when sprayed through a nozzle gun, creates fluffy snowdrifts that eventually evaporate.

Icicles are easily made by dripping strips of cellophane into melted paraffin and frosty windowpanes are the result of brushing on a mixture of Epsom salts (that's the stuff people put in hot water and use for soaking their sore feet) and very stale beer!

Creating frosty breath is a much thornier problem. One director actually filmed winter scenes in the storage room of a Los Angeles refrigerating company where the temperature was a bracing 15° Fahrenheit.

The special-effects artists working on one "snowbound" movie set devised tiny cages filled with dry ice that actors could hold inside their mouths. Obviously dialogue was impossible with these contraptions, but for shots where actors were seen trekking across the snow, they just had to breathe out naturally to produce steamy vaporized breath. Unfortunately one foolhardy actor grew fed up with all of the uncomfortable hardware, took out the cage, popped the dry ice back into his mouth, and burned his tongue and jaw very seriously.

Of all movies, probably the one that is most synonymous with cold and snow is *Dr. Zhivago* (1965), a sweeping screen spectacular

For **Dr.** Zhivago, *lots of marble-dust snow and realistic periods sets turned the outskirts of Madrid into turn-of-the-century Moscow. (Copyright 1965, MGM; Museum of Modern Art/Film Stills Archive)*

Creating artificial snow for this scene from The Invisible Man *was no problem, but making footprints appear out of nowhere was a tricky feat. A long board — with footprint shapes cut out of it and then replaced — was laid over a trench in the ground and then covered with artificial snow. Each footprint shape was hooked up to a rope which effects workers pulled, one at a time, and mysterious footprints appeared in the snow. (Copyright © Universal City Studios, Inc. All rights reserved.)*

about the Russian Revolution. Boris Pasternak's anti-Communist novel, on which the movie was based, was banned in the Soviet Union and, not surprisingly, not one foot of film was shot in the original locale. For deep snow and frosty breath the crew went to Finland, but most of the Arctic winter scenes were filmed in Spain — during the heat of summer. In the suburbs of Madrid a half-mile replica of turn-of-the-century Moscow was built, complete with the Kremlin and other architectural landmarks. The gigantic outdoor sets were very authentic looking — right down to the shop signs in

Cyrillic writing—and vast quantities of marble dust covered the streets of this mini-Moscow for convincing winter realism.

The crew also spent three months in northern Spain, where the terrain looked much like the bleak snow-covered steppes of Russia, and luckily the weather was cold enough in January for the cast to be comfortable wearing heavy overcoats and fur hats.

To frost actors' faces, a mixture of beaten egg whites and Epsom salts can be brushed on, but for an early comedy starring the silent-film star Harold Lloyd this effect was not enough. The plot, which involved hero and heroine being stuck in a refrigerator car of a train for two days, required that Lloyd and his costar be turned into living icicles. Their clothes had to look as if they had frozen solid.

For this tricky deep-freeze job, the special-effects man lined Lloyd's suit with a very heavy linen so that it looked stiff, painted on several layers of paraffin wax, then coated the clothes with clear rosin. Ironically, it was steaming hot inside this "icy" armor, which was also very difficult to get into—two men had to lift Lloyd up and gently lower him into his trousers, which were held by the special-effects man.

As for the costar's clothes, the special-effects man opted to forgo the laborious task of paraffin-painting her costume and instead soaked her dress in a substance called "liquid glass." According to legend, the result was wonderfully realistic, but the leading lady sneezed after getting into her dress and it shattered into a number of embarrassing pieces!

Whether or not this anecdote is true, it shows the ingenuity and effort special-effects men must use to produce weather effects that may only be on screen for a few seconds. And, with the exception of such spectacular scenes as the storm sequence in *The Hurricane*, these weather effects never even register in the minds of the audience—to moviegoers they simply look "as right as rain."

8

Familiar Faces: Makeup Effects

"The Man of 1,000 Faces"—that's what silent-screen star Lon Chaney was called because of his spectacular disguises in such classic horror movies as *Phantom of the Opera* (1925) and *The Hunchback of Notre Dame* (1923). Through complicated, often outlandish makeup tricks that he invented all by himself, Chaney was able to turn himself into a living, breathing special effect.

FEARSOME FACES

Skillful makeup techniques like Chaney's can create amazing illusions on film, although it's a hard job fooling the eagle eye of the camera. In the early days of film making, actors and actresses used the old standbys of stage performers—lots of greasepaint and powder. But what looked good on stage looked all wrong on screen. Stage makeup is applied very heavily and purposely exaggerated so that a performer's face and expressions can be clearly seen by theater-goers, even those in the top balconies. But a movie screen shows performers at several times their actual size (in close-up a face can be fifteen feet high!) so every bit of makeup trickery becomes easy to spot. Very, very artful techniques had to be developed, or else the

Lon Chaney, "The Man of 1,000 Faces," in two of his most famous guises: as the Phantom of the Opera and the Hunchback of Notre Dame. (Museum of Modern Art/Film Stills Archive)

ruthless lens of the camera would pick out the telltale line of a toupee or a nose obviously made out of putty.

The ghoulish guises that Chaney concocted more than fifty years ago are still considered marvels of realism, even by today's standards,

although the lengths to which he went to achieve his frightening illusions are downright alarming. Lon Chaney appeared in almost 150 films before his death in 1930, yet he always claimed that he hated being in the public eye. His makeup disguises certainly helped him hide from his fans. Many people had no idea what the real Chaney — minus all the makeup — looked like.

Chaney also tried his best to keep anyone from knowing how he achieved his startling makeup effects. One thing, however, is certain. Chaney suffered a great deal of pain to look grotesque on screen. For example, in one movie where he played a blind man, Chaney took the inner skin of an egg — the thin white covering that can be peeled off from inside an eggshell — and pressed it right over his eyeball. This did the trick of making his eye look cloudy and sightless, but it was excruciating painful for him and actually damaged his eye.

In *Phantom of the Opera*, one of Chaney's greatest hits, he portrayed a strange masked man who haunts the Paris Opera House and who falls in love with a young singer. The bone-chilling climax comes when the girl sneaks up behind "the Phantom" and pulls off his mask. What's revealed is a terrifying, scarred skull of a face that still makes audiences gasp.

How did Chaney do it? Well, that's a good question. Some film historians say he inserted little wires inside his nostrils and under his bottom eyelids to pull back his nose and bulge out his eyes. Others say he used tape to turn his nose up and keep his ears flattened against his head. It's certainly apparent that he used false teeth and some kind of skullcap with a stringy little wig. And he also seems to have used putty to build up his cheekbones and complete the "death mask" effect.

The highlight of Chaney's career, in terms of his acting as well as his makeup, came with his performance in *The Hunchback of Notre Dame*.

Chaney spent four and a half hours each day putting on his makeup and costume for Quasimodo, the deaf, hunchback bell ringer of Notre Dame Cathedral who falls in love with and ultimately gives his life for a young gypsy girl.

Chaney started out by strapping a 42-pound rubber hump onto his back. This hump was attached to a 30-pound leather harness that "shrunk" him to 4'1" (normally he was 5'10"). This harness contraption made moving around so painful that Chaney could stand to wear it only for fairly short periods of filming. Over the harness went a flesh-colored rubber suit covered with clumps of hair. Then Chaney contorted his face by sticking wax inside his mouth to puff out his cheeks and by placing putty over one eye. Uneven capped teeth, a wig, and medieval costume completed the grotesque yet strangely moving characterization. A reporter interviewing Chaney for *Photoplay Magazine* in 1928 summed it up when she wrote, "To endure pain for his work brought him strange joy."

Like Chaney, most silent-screen actors and actresses applied their own makeup, just as stage performers have always done. Yet as movie making became big and serious business, much greater attention was paid to how stars looked on screen. By the 1930s the major film studios each had their own makeup departments where professional cosmeticians worked their wonders. Yet except for the six famous Westmore brothers, who made it a practice to hobnob with the stars and who, at one time or another, headed the makeup depart-

The first film to receive an Academy Award for makeup was 7 Faces of Dr. Lao which is about a strange Chinese circus master who comes to a frontier town. Makeup artist Bill Tuttle created all the masks for star Tony Randall, who popped up in many guises throughout the movie. (Copyright © 1964, MGM; Museum of Modern Art/Film Stills Archive)

ments at Paramount, Universal, Warner Brothers, RKO, Twentieth Century-Fox, and other movie lots, makeup artists have been virtually unknown to the general public even though they have launched some of the most famous faces on the silver screen.

MAKEUP MARVELS

Interestingly enough, when Boris Karloff referred to "the true creator of horror men," he wasn't describing the evil Dr. Frankenstein. He was talking about a makeup artist, Jack Pierce, who turned Karloff into the most famous movie monster of all time.

Until his "transformation," Karloff had been pretty much unknown—a calm, cricket-playing Englishman who was born with the name of William Henry Pratt. Pierce changed all that, and the way he went about it proves that there was quite a bit of the "mad scientist" in him.

"I discovered there are six ways a surgeon can cut the skull," Pierce explained after the release of the horror movie classic, "and I figured Dr. Frankenstein, who was not a practicing surgeon, would take the easiest. That is, he would cut the top of the skull straight across like a pot lid, hinge it, pop the brain in, and clamp it tight. That's the reason I decided to make the Monster's head square and flat like a box."

To give Karloff's eyes a dumb, bewildered look, Pierce added strips of rubber onto his upper eyelids. Other spooky touches were black shoe polish on his fingernails and blue-green face paint, which on black-and-white film gave Karloff a sickly, ghostly look.

The best feature of Pierce's makeup was that it didn't hinder Karloff's acting in any way. He had full control of his expressions and gave a brilliant performance, making audiences sympathize with the pathetic doomed creature.

Frankenstein's monster has become so familiar, so much a part of our culture, that it's sometimes hard to realize that Pierce did not copy the famous face from anywhere. He had no pictures or photographs to follow—only Mary Shelley's description of the wretched creature in her book. The face of the monster was Pierce's own invention, dreamed up in his workshop. Dressing Room #5 on the Universal Studios lot. This was his laboratory, where he experimented and prepared his makeup effects—in complete privacy so

Boris Karloff in full regalia for Frankenstein. *(Copyright © Universal City Studios, Inc. All rights reserved.)*

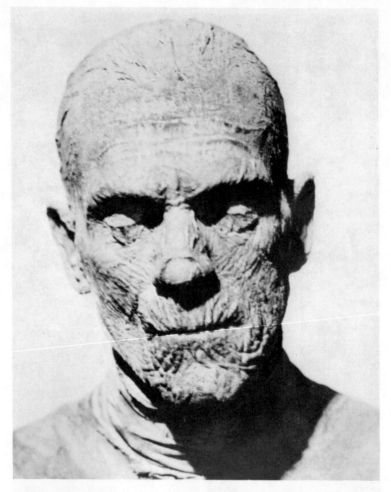

Mum's the word as to how makeup artist Jack Pierce really achieved this embalmed look for Boris Karloff in The Mummy. *(Copyright © Universal City Studios, Inc. All rights reserved.)*

none of his secrets could be stolen. It was there that he also created the stunning makeup effects for *The Mummy* (1932).

Mummy pictures became popular after the discovery of King Tut's tomb in 1922. For *The Mummy* which again starred Boris

Karloff, Pierce found a photograph of an actual Egyptian mummy and duplicated it. He explained at the time, "I used only threads of cotton so put on the face that they looked like creased flesh. First I made up a miniature head in clay, the way I wanted Karloff to look, then I modeled the same thing on Karloff and tested him. It took eight hours to put the full mummy makeup on him and then he worked six hours and it took two more hours to get it off. Fortunately he needed full makeup only one day."

It is hard to know whether Pierce was being completely honest or was protecting professional secrets. Other sources conflict with Pierce's own version of how he mummified Boris Karloff. Some film historians say that Karloff's face was covered with "beauty" mud and fuller's earth, then baked under hot-air driers.

Like Pierce, top movie cosmeticians today are not just called to make actors and actresses look good in front of the camera. They must also know how to perform tricky special-effects jobs such as "aging" a star fifty years in the course of a ninety-minute movie, showing the "victim" of a fire or a fistfight, and turning someone into the spitting image of Abraham Lincoln. Such special situations require very special makeup, but before explaining these complicated techniques, it's best to start out explaining simpler illusions created by makeup—the basic tricks of the trade.

BLOOD, SWEAT, AND TEARS

Getting right down to the gory details, ever since the earliest days of movie making, stars have been gushing, oozing, trickling, or dripping blood, as the case may be, on screen. Victims in silent movies "bled" chocolate syrup, which looked just like the real McCoy on the kind of black-and-white film used then. If a cowboy in a Western was to get shot, just before the scene was filmed a little chocolate syrup would be poured into the palm of his hand. Then, when the cameras started rolling and the cowboy got "blasted," he merely slapped his hand to his chest and what audiences saw was the bloody aftermath.

As improvements were made in black-and-white film so it could pick up subtle differences in tone, chocolate syrup looked much too dark and very phony. And, of course, with the introduction of color film, other "blood types" had to be found.

Today there are two basic kinds of movie blood, which are manufactured by makeup companies such as Max Factor: Panchromatic, a deep brownish-red artificial blood, is used for black-and-white movies while bright red Technicolor blood is used for color films. And not only are these chemically formulated types of blood ultra-realistic (they dry and crust just like the real thing), they are also washable and nonstaining, important considerations when expensive costumes are being used.

Fake sweat is another staple makeup effect. After all, how many performers can perspire on cue? A fairly good sweat can be worked up simply by spraying an actor with an atomizer of water. The only problem is that water dries quickly under hot movie-studio lights. Longer-lasting beads of sweat are created by mixing a solution of glycerin (a thick, clear liquid) and water. Atomizers, by the way are used so that makeup artists can control the amount of perspiration—they can spray on just a little for a slight trickle or lots for a virtual downpour.

While no director can reasonably expect a performer to perspire at will, there are some actors and actresses who can cry on command. Katharine Hepburn, for one, is famous for her talent at summoning up tears. But most actors must rely on glycerin tears inserted with an eyedropper right before an emotional scene.

Real tears can be stimulated by breaking a little vial of spirits of ammonia and having the performer breathe in the fumes. Just like being near a freshly cut raw onion, this produces red, watery eyes.

HAIR TODAY, GONE TOMORROW

What self-respecting pirate movie would ever have a clean-shaven captain? And just where would the Wolfman be without a face full of fuzz? Many different kinds of scripts call for a character to be bearded. Yet an actor may not have enough time to grow a real beard before filming starts or, in the case of the Wolfman, an actor could have all the time in the world and never get sufficiently hairy on his own. For these and other situations, the practical solution is fake beards.

For today's movies, beards and moustaches are almost always made from *real-hair crepe*, which is either human hair or yak hair (yes, yak hair—it's very realistic looking) or a combination of the two. Real-hair crepe comes in a braid and is available in many colors.

After the clumps of real-hair crepe have been glued to a performer's face with spirit gum (a clear, brown glue that's very strong), they can be trimmed to whatever shape beard the makeup artist wants.

Of course, it's very hard for a makeup artist to duplicate a beard exactly, so this technique isn't used if a performer has to appear bearded for more than a day or two of filming. Instead, reusable hair-pieces are used. These are moustaches, beards, eyebrows, sideburns . . . even chest wigs, which were used a lot in the 1920s to make he-men stars look more macho. Professional wigmakers make hairpieces by hand-sewing real hair onto lace netting. The lace netting is so fine that, when glued onto the performer's face, it's really invisible. The makeup artist just has to be careful not to tear the delicate lace when removing a hairpiece. This way it can be used again and again.

THE BALD FACTS

Short of shaving an actor's head — and most performers feel that this is above and beyond the call of duty — the most effective way of showing baldness is to glue a paper-thin rubber cap on over the per-former's head. After the actor's hair has been slicked back or pinned up, the cap is slipped over the head. A bald cap fits like a tight bathing cap and is very strong and stretchable. It can be glued down with liquid latex, a milky-white liquid that dries into a skin-like elas-tic material, and then blended to the performer's skin with makeup.

Interestingly enough, one performer who decided to forgo the bald cap and face the razor was a woman. Bald female roles are few and far between, but in *The Private Lives of Elizabeth and Essex,* (1939) Bette Davis had the starring role of Queen Elizabeth the First of England. The sixteenth-century monarch was never noted for her looks. She didn't have any eyebrows and, as she grew older, her hairline receded further and further. When it came time for her makeup, Bette Davis opted for total realism and gave the go-ahead to shave her eyebrows as well as the whole front half of her head (the rest was covered with a bright-red wig just like the one the real Elizabeth wore).

SCAR-IFYING EFFECTS

Scars are a snap for makeup artists. Well-healed ones are made by brushing on collodion, which looks and smells like colorless nail polish. When it dries, it pulls and puckers the skin into a realistic scar. Deeper, nastier scars call for several layers of collodion. Then, as soon as the scar dries, it can be colored with maroon makeup for a raw, angry look. Gorgeous!

TRIAL BY FIRE

Scorching, burning, or charring actors is a somewhat trickier business, but a talented makeup artist can produce anything from small blisters to massive burns.

For a truly charcoaled look, liquid latex is first applied. When it dries, little bits of it are picked off to look like peeling skin. Maroon makeup is dabbed on unevenly around the peeling area, then blisters can be made by dripping plain old white candle wax in small blobs onto the latex. Lastly, black liquid makeup can also be dabbed around the "burn."

THE RAVAGES OF TIME

It's a fact that the old saying "Time waits for no man" is almost as true on screen as it is in real life. Makeup artists are not magicians, and they can only do so much to make a performer look younger: gray hair can be dyed, toupees can hide a receding hairline, the rosy glow of youth can be restored via rouge, wrinkles can be masked to some degree by makeup (then further erased by the cameraman, who shoots an aging star slightly out of focus or places gauze over the lens for a softer, blurrier effect). Then, too, there are special cases, as with child star Shirley Temple, who was kept "young" by wearing false front teeth after her baby ones fell out! Still, it's just a matter of degree; a performer getting on in years can be made up to look younger, but not young.

On the other hand, there's no problem at all speeding up the ravages of time. Makeup artists can really pull all the stops out and achieve mind-boggling old-age effects.

In some respects, making a performer look just a little older is harder than making someone look ancient, because the changes are such subtle ones and they must look that way on screen. Wrinkles, for example, are made with liquid latex: the makeup artist stretches the performer's skin and dabs on liquid latex with a sponge. When the latex dries, more is dabbed on and allowed to dry. Then this tightly stretched area of skin is powdered and pinched together by the makeup artist to create convincing wrinkles.

Gray hair, another telltale sign of advancing years, can be achieved either by using permanent hair dyes or, if a part requires gray hair for only a day or two of shooting, by spraying on silver hair spray.

PHONY NOSES, RUBBER NECKS

For a makeup artist to transform a performer into a doddering old-timer, latex wrinkles and gray hair are simply not enough. Jowls, bags under the eyes, sagging neck skin (appropriately called turkey wattles), a drooping nose, and gnarled hands are all part and parcel of old age.

But there is no way to paint on any of these features, so instead makeup artists use artificial jowls, bags, et cetera made out of liquid latex or other rubbery substances that can be made to resemble skin. Artificial features are called *prosthetics* or *appliances*. They are not just used for dramatic aging; they are also indispensable in creating

The piece-by-piece application of rubber appliances shows how actress Kim Hunter "went ape" in Planet of the Apes. *(1967, Twentieth Century-Fox)*

makeup for monsters, for famous historical figures, and for any other role in which a performer's own features will have to be changed.

In the film *Little Big Man* (1970) which follows the long, up-and-down life of a jack-of-all-trades frontiersman, the star, Dustin Hoffman, who was 33 at the time of filming, had to be aged from a young boy to an incredibly old man of 121.

Makeup artist Dick Smith, who masterminded the transformation of Dustin Hoffman, researched and tested out each phase of the job thoroughly. Long before the actual filming started Smith visited a home for the aged, where he was able to observe how very old people looked and acted. He also consulted his own extensive collection of photographs, which he had built up over the years, to get an idea of the kind of face he wanted.

"What you must remember," Smith said in a published interview, "is that aging presents a delicate problem; some people in their late 80's look older than people over 100. When people reach very advanced ages, it's because their rate of aging has been slower than the normal person's. So I had to find some way to indicate this extraordinary age. If you just continued the normal aging process in arithmetical proportions, something like x years equals x wrinkles, you'd have a decayed corpse look."

Smith wanted to try out many different effects to create his aged character. Like many makeup artists, he used modeling clay to build up a hooknose, a knotted forehead, whatever. And what he modeled on was the actor's face.

About now you're probably thinking that no actor is going to sit around for days while a makeup artist sticks clay on him and turns him into a living sculpture.

You're right! What the makeup artist does instead is to make a plaster model of the actor's face — an exact likeness on which he can experiment and which is far better than the living, breathing actor, since it never complains and always keeps perfectly still.

Having a plaster model made is no picnic for a performer. A thick coating of a fast-hardening cream — very often the cream that dentists use to take an impression of your teeth — is put on over the performer's entire face. (Straws are inserted in the nostrils so that the actor can keep on breathing and make it to the first day of filming!) Then wet plaster-of-Paris bandages are laid on top of the impression cream.

All during this time the performer cannot move a muscle. After thirty long minutes, everything is dry and the mask can be lifted off. This mask or shell is then placed like a bowl on a table and filled with plaster of Paris. When it is dry, the plaster is separated from the shell. The plaster is now a perfect replica of the performer's face. Now the makeup artist can fool around as much as he wants to with his modeling clay, finding the right features for his creation.

In the case of the 121-year-old character in *Little Big Man* once Dick Smith had sculpted the perfect features onto the plaster model, individual molds of each fake feature had to be made. From these molds the actual latex appliances were created.

Individual appliances — a nose, an ear, etc. — can be molded in several ways. One way is for a makeup artist to sculpt the desired feature — a hooknose, for example — on top of the nose on the plaster model. Then a "well" of clay is built around the clay hooknose. Plaster is poured to the top of the well. When the plaster is dry and hard, the clay well is removed. The resulting plaster nose mold is then eased off the plaster model of the performer's face and the clay hooknose that the makeup artist sculpted is removed from the inside of the mold.

What's left is a perfect mold of the hooknose, from which the makeup artist can create a nose appliance. He does this by taking liquid latex and painting several thin coatings of it inside the mold. After the latex is dry, the latex hooknose is carefully peeled out of the mold.

Once a makeup artist has a mold, he can make as many noses as are needed. A complete set of noses and all other appliances will be needed for each day of filming that the actor will be in his makeup. (The appliances get torn when they're removed, so they can only be used once.) Appliances can also be made months beforehand and stockpiled until the film production begins.

As for *Little Big Man* there were two special things about the makeup that Smith eventually designed after three months of hard work. First of all, a bald cap was not used; instead, appliances of latex covered Dustin Hoffman's whole head. This was so the skull would also have wrinkles and veins and give the suggestion of bones underneath. The few little bits of hair were punched in by hand, one by one.

Secondly, the eyelid pieces were very remarkable. Usually these pieces can't move, so a performer must keep his eyes open all during the time of filming. If he blinks, his real eyelids will come out from under them. But Smith made pieces that were so thin that they could move with the real eyelids.

Another interesting fact is that all of the appliances were pre-painted with tiny little age spots and veins months before shooting. This helped to save time when Dustin Hoffman had to be made up. Even so, it took Smith five hours each day to apply Hoffman's makeup. First each feature had to be positioned on Hoffman's face and glued on with spirit gum. Then liquid latex was painted around the edges to blend the appliance in with Hoffman's real skin.

The end result was so successful that people on the set began treating Hoffman like an old man. They would help him out of his chair and offer him an arm to lean on. Dustin Hoffman even began to feel like a very old man, which undoubtedly helped his performance a great deal.

MAKEUP MASKS

Sometimes a performer's entire face is covered with appliances until a complete mask is created. That is what happened to Kim Hunter, Roddy McDowall, and all the other simian stars of *Planet of the Apes*(1967).

John Chambers was the makeup artist responsible for the remarkable man-to-monkey transformations. He got his training in making appliances during World War II. As an army technician, he learned how to make plastic or rubber noses, ears, and other lifelike features for soldiers whose faces had been disfigured in battle. This training proved invaluable when Chambers was selected to design and produce the makeup effects for *Planet of the Apes*.

The movie is about a crew of astronauts (led by Charlton Heston) who land on Earth in the distant future when apes rule the world. It cost six million dollars to make, with a whopping one million dollars spent on makeup.

One of the first problems Chambers faced was finding the right kind of rubber out of which to make the appliances. The first compounds that were tried were too tough and stiff. When all of the mask pieces were tried out on some human test cases, they did not look lifelike at all. They looked more like wax masks. Even the worse,

The end result of John Chambers' handiwork for Planet of the Apes *won him an Oscar for makeup effects. (1967, Twentieth Century-Fox)*

the people couldn't move their faces underneath all of the heavy rubber makeup.

After much experimenting, Chambers and a team of chemists and makeup experts came up with a new rubber compound that wasn't too stiff and that would stretch as the actors moved their faces. If, for example, an ape actor had to speak, the lips of the mask would form the words the same way as real lips would. (The new rubber compound also let performers' skin breathe, which, when actual production began, made life much easier for the monkey actors, since the film was shot in Arizona with temperatures reaching a sizzling 120 degrees.)

After finding the right rubber for the masks, Chambers had to find the right design for the ape faces. Originally he thought that the actors would breathe through the nostrils of the nose appliances. This was fine for breathing, but not good for creating a realistic-looking ape face. That's because a monkey's nose sits much higher on the face than a human nose. So Chambers raised the position of the nose on the mask, then made a slit in the upper-lip piece through which an actor could breathe.

Lastly there was a problem of time. At first it took makeup artists six to seven hours to put all of the pieces of each mask on an actor and three hours to peel them all off. What Chambers did was to hire an army of makeup specialists who, through teamwork and practice, managed to cut the entire time of applying and removing the masks to four and a half hours. For crowd scenes with two hundred "ape" extras, so many makeup people were needed that production was stalled on other movies and television shows being filmed at the same time. All the time and effort, however, paid off for Twentieth Century-Fox. *Planet of the Apes* was so popular that four sequels have been made.

For the famous cantina scene in *Star Wars*, where a motley assortment of odd-looking aliens listen attentively to an outer-space jazz combo, the makeup crew didn't have enough time to make individual appliances for the faces of the various species of galactic lowlife. Instead, one-piece rubber head masks were used, not unlike the ones sold in toystores at Halloween.

Originally a British makeup expert named Stuart Freeborn was to create the effects makeup for the spaceport creatures. It was Freeborn who came up with the yak-hair costume of the towering, apelike Wookie. But while *Star Wars* was being filmed in the deserts of Tunisia, Freeborn became ill and left his assistants to create the makeup for the cantina scene.

Director George Lucas was far from pleased with the results. He felt that the aliens looked too much like the hairy animal types seen in lots of Grade B sci-fi flicks. The scene was shot, but months later, still brooding over the poor effects, Lucas hired makeup artist Rick Baker, fresh from his work on Dino De Laurentiis'*King Kong*, to give the aliens a "face-lift."

Normally it would take Baker about six weeks to construct one creature, but for *Star Wars* he and his team of assistants had six weeks to design and make the molds for about twenty masks and pairs of hands. Because it was such a rush job, Baker's crew decided to make slit-rubber masks out of latex which could just slip over the actors' heads. The masks had slits or ventilation holes near the mouth so that the performers could breathe.

All of the footage of Baker and company's aliens was shot in one

Makeup artist Rick Baker poses with some of the space creatures he created for Star Wars. *(Photo copyright © 1979 Arthur Sirdofsky)*

day and inserted into the sequence done by Stuart Freeborn. Rick Baker was not terribly pleased with the results. "Since we only had six weeks and a limited budget, we could not do anything outstanding or complicated," he told reporters. "Old masks that had been sitting on my shelf for years were thrown in the day they were shot as filler for the background. Much to my dismay, they ended up being very much in the foreground. One in particular was a crummy werewolf mask that I made as a mass-production item!" Movie fans, however, were not disappointed; the comic cantina scene turned out to be one of the high points of the film.

The imaginative effects work in such movies as *Planet of the Apes* and *Star Wars* shows that it's a mistake to think that all a makeup artist does is choose the right shade of lipstick for an actress or find ways to cover up a teen screen idol's blemishes. And although makeup work may not normally be considered a true part of special effects, the pros who experiment with molds and masks have nevertheless achieved some of the most unforgettable illusions on screen.

9

WRAPPING IT UP

If Méliès, by means of the ultimate special effect, could come back today and take a look at what has happened in films since his time, almost eighty years ago, he'd probably feel a kinship to director George Lucas and his group of effects aces, who created the outer-space illusions for *Star Wars* in a huge warehouse aptly named Industrial Light and Magic. And no doubt he'd feel proud that many of the optical effects, action props, and even miniatures used today are not so very different from the ones he pioneered in his magic-show movies.

Yet even though his trick films were all the rage for a while, Méliès died penniless. Audiences had grown tired of all the "presto chango" tricks and dazzling but meaningless special effects. They wanted something more; they wanted a story.

It was Edwin Porter, an American, who first saw that special effects were most effective when they helped make an exciting story more real. Porter's *The Great Train Robbery* (1903) had about as many cinematic tricks as Méliès films, but they were used to add to the adventure and keep the audience on the edge of their seats.

From the turn of the century through most of the 1920s, movie making was pretty much a freewheeling, casual endeavor. Stars, like daredevil comdeian Buster Keaton, often performed dangerous stunts themselves. Camera operators were responsible for optical trickery, such as undercranking, overcranking, and making special

Early effects from magician Georges Méliès: a lunar landing and lovely moon maidens from A Trip to the Moon. *(Museum of Modern Art/Film Stills Archive)*

Outlaws in Porter's The Great Train Robbery *hold up a telegraph office. The train seen through the office window is the first matte shot ever used in a movie that told a story. (Museum of Modern Art/Film Stills Archive)*

cutout matte cards—a heart-shaped one to frame lovers in a kissing scene or a binocular-shaped matte to indicate someone peering into the distance. Physical effects—trapdoor disappearances or flash-powder explosions—were done by anyone handy on the production crew. There simply were no such things as specialists.

Then, almost overnight, the whole film industry was turned upside down, and all because an actor named Al Jolson sang on screen —and the audience heard the lyrics. *The Jazz Singer* (1927) ushered in a new era in movie making—the Talkies. In the days of the Silent Screen, movies had been shot freely out of doors amid roaring traffic and screaming directors. Now location shooting had to be abandoned. Everything was done inside studio sets where even camera motors had to be muffled in huge soundproof booths or else the noise would be picked up by the new sound equipment.

But while camera operators bemoaned their loss of mobility, the changeover to sound gave rise to a whole new branch of film making — the Special Effects Department. As is often the case, necessity was the mother of invention. With film crews locked inside sound stages, the outside world had to be re-created on the studio set. And, of course, it was up to the special-effects men to carry off the trickery. By the early 1930s, each major studio had its own special-effects department with professional wizards who specialized in making miniatures or building action props or performing optical illusions.

Movies in the Roaring Twenties reflected the trends of the day. War movies, slapstick comedy, Westerns, romances, and cliff-hanger thrillers were the people's choice in film fare. But the 1930s saw a switch in moviegoers' tastes that also tested the ingenuity of the new special-effects crews. During the Great Depression, audiences looked to movies as an escape from hard times. They wanted to see lush, gorgeous musical extravaganzas like *42nd Street* (1933) and *Footlight Parade* (1933) and all the other Busby Berkeley spectaculars. They also flocked to see thriller fantasies like *Dracula* (1931), *King Kong* (1933), *Frankenstein* (1931), and *The Invisible Man* (1933). Oddly enough, audiences also crowded in to see disaster movies like *The Rains Came* (1939) and *The Hurricane* (1937) which evidently made real life, with its rampant unemployment and long breadlines, seem not quite so bad by comparison.

During this time, Special Effects Departments became so good that their work became "invisible." Audiences could no longer tell what was real and what was faked. Even in the 1940s, when sound equipment became portable and film crews could once again emerge from the studios, many directors preferred to stay right where they were. They had learned that the environment could be controlled inside the studio, and they weren't about to give up their made-to-order world so quickly.

Then, too, the outbreak of World War II severely limited location work. War epics were churned out at an amazing rate, but since no film crews could travel to Normandy or Pearl Harbor to film real battle scenes, it was up to the special-effects experts to stage the war-fare with miniature planes, non-lethal "bombs," and "casualties" who never stayed dead for very long.

In the 1950s, the war had ended and the space race between the United States and Russia had begun. The infant space program opened up new worlds beyond and suddenly everyone was asking, "Is there life on Mars?" Naturally, Hollywood didn't let such an opportunity go to waste. A rash of sci-fi movies were released—*When Worlds Collide* (1951), *War of the Worlds* (1953), *Forbidden Planet* (1956), *Invasion of the Body Snatchers* (1956), and many more. They catered to the national paranoia about invading aliens and kept special-effects crews busy making model spaceships and assorted beasts from other worlds.

Ironically, it was during he 1950s that a one-eyed monster *did* invade the country—and nearly spelled the end of movies. The monster, of course, was television. Suddenly, everyone was staying home to watch—for free—flickering images on tiny black-and-white

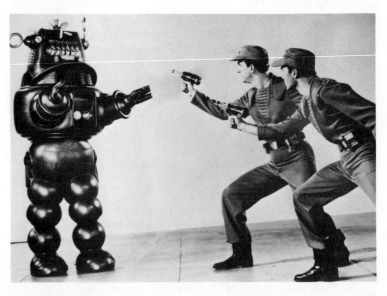

Robbie the Robot startles space explorers from Earth in the 1950s sci-fi classic Forbidden Planet. *(MGM, 1956; Museum of Modern Art/Film Stills Archive)*

screens. Movie houses were empty and the major studios were on the verge of ruin.

In an effort to top the tube, film producers tired to lure back audiences with gimmicks, such as extra wide-screen Cinerama, 3-D movies for which viewers wore special glasses that made the action seem to pop out from the screen, and even a process — called, not surprisingly, Smell-O-Vision — whereby odors were wafted through the theater.

None of these gimmicks really did the trick of successfully competing with TV, so a new strategy had to be found. By the beginning of the 1960s, moviemakers reached the conclusion that the one thing television couldn't do was film on-the-scene action. TV crews at that time were in much the same spot as movie crews of the early 1930s; because of heavy equipment, they had to stay within the confines of the studio. Film makers quickly abandoned their studios and began going on location to all sorts of exotic places. No more were rear projection or matte paintings used to provide background scenery. Realism was the operative word. Moviemakers were proud if they could claim that there wasn't one optically faked shot in their films.

In *Grand Prix* (1966), for example, which is a car-racing movie shot on location in Italy, the director refused to use any miniatures for scenes of crashing cars. Instead, he used an "air cannon" which "shot" actual cars — minus their heavy engines — hurtling on a crash course at speeds of up to a hundred miles per hour.

This surge in realism meant steady employment for stunt people who were willing to risk their necks for a price, but for effects people, times were lean. On top of this trend toward realism, the Hollywood studio system was falling apart. Studios could no longer afford to keep large effects departments on the payroll. Just as the studios gave way to independent producers, special-effects departments gave way to free-lance effects workers who were hired on a one-job-at-a-time basis.

Then, strangely enough, the recession-ridden seventies put moviemakers back on their feet and special-effects men were back in business. Just as in the 1930s, people lined up to see the new flood of disaster movies. First to be released was *The Poseidon Adventure* (1972) — the story of survivors on board a capsized ocean liner — followed in quick succession by such box-office blockbusters as *Earthquake* (1974), *Towering Inferno* (1974), and, of course, *Jaws* (1974). All of a

In direct contrast to most of the realistic movies of the 1960s was Kubrick's 2001: A Space Odyssey, which dazzled audiences with its optical and mechanical effects. Here, a stewardess defies gravity in a slick spaceship. (Copyright © 1968, MGM)

sudden, effects men, who had all but retired during the realistic sixties, were called back into action to create these catastrophic flicks.

It was not until 1977, however, when the megahit *Star Wars* blazed across movie screens, that special effects actually became the star attraction of a movie. *Star Wars* was followed quickly by *Close Encounters of the Third Kind* (1977), *Superman* (1978), and a remake of *Invasion of the Body Snatchers* (1978). Starting with *Star Wars* it was not unheard of for a movie such as *Star Trek—The Motion Picture* (1979) to have up to 50 per cent of its entire budget spent on special effects. A new Golden Age of special effects had arrived.

As for the future of special effects, who knows? Experiments are already being done with holograms, truly three-dimensional images that move so that viewers can see a film from all sides and angles, and even walk around it to see what the images look like from the other side. Interestingly enough, the problem with bringing out hologram movies is not so much one of perfecting the technology but one of building movie theaters with special seating and projection equipment to let audiences properly experience this illusion of the third dimension.

Then again, special effects may no longer be limited to the movies. Optical wizards like John Dykstra and Douglas Trumbull have begun to create effects for other entertainment media like amusement parks and discos. Rock groups now hire effects experts so that they can land at their concerts in glowing rocketships or dazzle fans by materializing from explosive clouds of smoke. But such spectacular effects don't come cheap. Maybe movie producers will begin to make "small" movies again—movies like *Breaking Away* (1979), for example—that tell a good old-fashioned screen story but require few effects are easier on the budget.

No matter what the next chapter in the saga of special effects may be, one thing is certain: we would never have had King Kong, Dracula, Bruce the Shark, Superman, a Planet of Apes, the Wolf Man, Darth Vader, or Godzilla become so vividly alive as our "folk heroes" without the cinemagic of the past.

Appendix: The Academy Awards for Special Effects

Year	Winning Movie
1927–28	*Wings* (Award for "Engineering Effects")
————	No awards were given from 1929 through 1938.
1939	*The Rains Came*
1940	*The Thief of Bagdad*
1941	*I Wanted Wings*
1942	*Reap the Wild Wind*
1943	*Crash Dive*
1944	*Thirty Seconds Over Tokyo*
1945	*Wonder Man*
1946	*Blithe Spirit*
1947	*Green Dolphin Street*
1948	*Portrait of Jennie*
1949	*Mighty Joe Young*
1950	*Destination Moon*
1951	*When Worlds Collide*
1952	*Plymouth Adventure*
1953	*War of the Worlds*
1954	*20,000 Leagues Under the Sea*
1955	*The Bridges at Toko-Ri*
1956	*The Ten Commandments*
1957	*The Enemy Below*
1958	*Tom Thumb*
1959	*Ben Hur*
1960	*The Time Machine*
1961	*The Guns of Navarone*
1962	*The Longest Day*

1963   *Cleopatra*
1964   *Mary Poppins*
1965   *Thunderball*
1966   *Fantastic Voyage*
1967   *Dr. Dolittle*
1968   *2001: A Space Odyssey*
1969   *Marooned*
1970   *Tora! Tora! Tora!*
1971   *Bedknobs and Broomsticks*
1972   *The Poseidon Adventure*
1973   No award given.
1974   *Earthquake*
1975   *The Hindenburg*
1976   *King Kong*
1977   *Star Wars*
1978   *Superman*

Bibliography

The following magazines and books have more information about movies with special effects:

Cinefantastique. Published quarterly. P.O. Box 270, Oak Part, Illinois, 60303.

AYLESWORTH, THOMAS G. *Movie Monsters*. Philadelphia and New York: J. B. Lippincott Company, 1975.

BOJARSKI, RICHARD, and BEALS, KENNETH. *The Films of Boris Karloff*. Secaucus, New Jersey: The Citadel Press, 1974.

EDELSON, EDWARD. *Great Monsters of the Movies*. New York: Doubleday & Company, Inc. 1973.

———. *Great Movie Spectaculars*. New York: Doubleday & Company, Inc. 1976.

GOLDNER, ORVILLE, and TURNER, GEORGE E. *The Making of King Kong*. New York: A. S. Barnes & Co., 1975.

McCLELLAND, DOUG. *Down the Yellow Brick Road: The Making of* The Wizard of Oz. New York: Pyramid Publications, Inc. 1976.

Index

Hans Christian Andersen was the first movie JANE O'CONNOR ever saw, and from the moment the theater darkened, she was hooked. A graduate of Smith College, Jane O'Connor is a children's book editor and reviewer who has written for *The New York Times Book Review*. Ms. O'Connor and her husband live in New York City with their baby son.

Katy Hall often spent her weekly allowance at the Shady Oak Theater while growing up in St. Louis, Missouri. Following a teaching career in California, Ms. Hall moved to Europe, made several short Super-8 movies, and taught film making to kids. She is now a free-lance writer and lives with her husband in New York City, where she frequently attends double features at the Regency.